CASSIE SUMNER

Loving It

**SHE'S THE MOST TALKED-ABOUT MODEL IN THE COUNTRY.
SHE'S DATED EVERYONE FROM RUSSELL BRAND TO MICHAEL ESSIEN.
THIS IS HER AMAZING TRUE STORY.**

G000069275

JB

JOHN BLAKE

Published by John Blake Publishing Ltd,
3 Bramber Court, 2 Bramber Road,
London W14 9PB, England

www.blake.co.uk

First published in hardback in 2008

ISBN: 978-1-84454-554-4

All rights reserved. No part of this publication may be reproduced,
stored in a retrieval system, or in any form or by any means, without
the prior permission in writing of the publisher, nor be otherwise circulated
in any form of binding or cover other than that in which it is published
and without a similar condition including this condition being imposed
on the subsequent publisher.

British Library Cataloguing-in-Publication Data:

A catalogue record for this book is available from the British Library.

Design by www.envydesign.co.uk

Printed in the UK by CPI William Clowes Beccles NR34 7TL

1 3 5 7 9 10 8 6 4 2

© Text copyright Cassie Sumner/Emma Bussey

Papers used by John Blake Publishing are natural, recyclable products
made from wood grown in sustainable forests. The manufacturing processes
conform to the environmental regulations of the country of origin.

Every attempt has been made to contact the relevant copyright-holders,
but some were unobtainable. We would be grateful if the appropriate people
could contact us.

Contents

Acknowledgements

I want to thank my family for their support and for sticking by me through thick and thin. I know it hasn't been easy for them, but everything they did for me during my journey has always been much appreciated and will never be forgotten. I want to thank my mother and my brother Ben for their undying love and care, without which I don't know if I'd have survived to tell my story. I also want to thank my dear stepfather Patrick, who has supported and nurtured me like his very own child. Without him, my life would feel incomplete.

In writing this book I may upset and disappoint some very important loved ones in my life. For me, it was a huge decision to talk about my past and, although it took a vast amount of courage to do so, I hope to God that the people I care about will look beyond any poor decisions I made and appreciate the woman that I have finally become. My life story may also shock those around me and some may not be able to accept some of the choices that I made, but I want those people to know that I have grown and have learned from my mistakes, and that my future is bright and filled with great promise and goodwill towards them.

Finally, I hold no grudges against the people who have hurt and mistreated me. I have learned to forgive and fully understand that as human beings we can easily fall prey to the negative aspects of the difficult world we live in. I am just thankful that I am able to finally speak out and in so doing can help others out there who may be faced with the same life-changing and often damaging choices as me.

Introduction

'Why aren't you joining in, Cassie?' the celebrity slurred. In one hand he was clenching a small glass pipe and in the other a battered lighter. I immediately recognised the sweet smell on his breath as we sat together on the velvet designer sofa. But when he pulled the small package of crack out of his expensive Prada wallet, I felt fear and disgust. 'I need to get out of here,' I replied, shaking my head at him. 'I can't bear to be amongst these people any more,' I said angrily, as I looked around the smoky, crowded hotel suite. The once pristine room was now awash with models, footballers and celebrities, all of them sinking bottles of champagne and snorting cocaine in an ugly, debauched display.

The man's girlfriend lay slumped beside him. She looked lifeless, but her eyeballs were rolling and their whites had turned yellow. Her frail hands were clutching a small piece of burned tin foil, which she'd used for her last hit of heroin. I thought I recognised her face from the modelling world, but I could have been mistaken. The smoke from the celebrity's pipe suddenly began to circle around me. I started to panic, but when I tried to stand up my feet felt like rocks. Next to the sofa was a large glass table. In its centre a pyramid of finely chopped cocaine had tempted a leggy model. She stooped over it and scooped up the powder using one of her perfectly manicured fingernails. She inhaled the drug through her tiny nostril and when it hit her bloodstream she flashed a knowing smile at me. Holding her head up high, she sauntered off into the thick of the party.

I peered helplessly through the billowing smoke over to the other side of the suite. A Premiership footballer had caught my eye because he was frantically kissing a petite young girl. His large tanned hands were moving quickly over her small, fragile frame. I couldn't see her face because another footballer came and stood in front of them. When the girl moaned in ecstasy, the two footballers began smiling at one another. Another player then joined in.

'What are you doing here, Cassie? Are you OK, sweetheart?' asked my father.

I couldn't see his face or answer him because the smoke had started to engulf me. As tears filled my stinging eyes, I could feel the words struggling with one another at the base of my throat. I knew they would only find their way out if I saw the outline of Papa's face, but the smoke was slowly beginning to suffocate me.

'It's me, Cassie. It's Papa,' I heard him cry.

'Have you come to take me away from here, Papa?

Introduction

Please, Papa, can't you take me somewhere nice? The smoke is killing me!' I replied, choking, while praying that my father would help me out of the hellish room.

'You're having a bad dream,' Lee said, as I opened my eyes.

'I'm fine,' I responded, as the fear within me subsided.

'Why don't you try to go back to sleep? I'm next to you, so don't worry,' he said, kissing me softly.

But I couldn't go back to sleep. Bad memories often come back to haunt me at night and it's then that I'm at my most vulnerable. My boyfriend Lee tells me that sometimes I cry in my sleep too. I know that when I'm asleep I dream about my past; I dream about missing Papa and feeling isolated. I dream about the bullying I suffered and the difficulties with men that I have endured. I dream about how tough it was when I began my modelling career and the mistakes I made along the way. I also dream about the decadent London party scene that I wholeheartedly dived into – and when I took immense risks with drugs.

As I lay there and thought about my past, I noticed that the light from the moon outside had found its way through a crack in the curtains and had settled itself on the ceiling. As the light began to dance happily above me, I suddenly thought of all the magical and glamorous times I'd enjoyed along the way. I'd also experienced so many life-changing and challenging moments that allowed me to rediscover 'me'. Through much hardship and learning I knew that I'd finally become a strong, independent and successful woman. I glanced over at Lee, who was now sound asleep next to me. I thought how lucky I was to have discovered our love and how that unconditional love had opened up a part of my heart that I'd never known existed. At last I felt secure and had a real sense of belonging with someone.

But that night, despite my inner strength and happiness, I still felt incomplete and as if I needed to find peace within me. I wanted to wake up the next day and feel a part of life, and to give something back too. That night, I realised that it was time for me to follow a new path that involved creating a process of change. I wanted other young models to hear my voice and so find guidance and comfort during their daunting journey into the unknown. Through my own words, I wanted to show them how they might avoid making the same mistakes that I'd made, and to reassure them that there's a very bright light at the end of their tunnel. That night I knew that I also needed to find closure with my past, that I had to lay to rest the nagging rumours that blighted my career and so by speaking my truth I knew that I could perhaps find a lasting peace within me.

As my eyes started to close, I felt clarity and release. The next morning I woke up feeling clear-headed and full of energy. I then began to write.

Chapter One

Daddy's Girl

WHEN I CAME INTO THE WORLD, MUM SAYS THAT SHE AND PAPA WERE MADLY IN LOVE. They'd happily planned their first child and, when I was born at Chichester Hospital in Hampshire on 13 January 1983, they were still enjoying their first year of marriage. I was named Cassandra Louise Muñoz and was very much a welcome little addition to their lives.

Even though I was born prematurely, I was healthy and strong. Soon after I arrived Mum and Papa moved back to the island of Menorca in Spain, where my father grew up, and where they had settled a year beforehand – I only happened to be born in England because they came over to visit my grandparents when Mum went into labour with me! Menorca is still a favourite choice among Brits who want to emigrate and it's also a popular tourist destination. Mum and Papa chose the island, though, because that was where they had met and fallen in love. Similarly, I feel a connection with Spain and would love to settle down there eventually. The natives are caring and very family orientated, but there's also something deeper within me that often draws me to it.

Regardless of the Spanish culture and my future hopes and aspirations, I feel such warmth when I imagine the beginning of my childhood there. Nan tells me my feelings are spot-on because I was so happy when Papa, Mum and I were together in Menorca. She says that, during my first year, my father Pepe was loving, protective and responsible, and that my mum – Karen – was happy caring for her family. Even though money was sparse, they both made the most of what they had and they gave me the best start they possibly could to my life.

As soon as we arrived on the island, Papa bought a small, cosy apartment in the village of Villa Carlos. We settled in quickly and happily and Papa started up a local car-hire company for the tourists. Mum says he was so content during those early days. He was extremely satisfied running his own business and was not only head over heels in love with her, but he very much doted on his new little girl. 'You were the apple of your father's eye, you were both inseparable,' Mum has told me many a time.

Every day someone would catch Papa pushing me in my pram up the steep, cobbled road to our little apartment, forever the proudest father around. I am told it was my almond-shaped brown eyes that captured everyone's heart, especially my father, and that he would love showing me off to all his friends. 'This is my gorgeous Cassie!' he'd beam, smothering my head in kisses. 'Isn't she the most beautiful baby girl? Just look at those pretty little eyes!'

'Yes, Pepe, simply adorable,' they would all coo and nod as they huddled excitedly around my pram.

Although of course I always loved Mum, my family says that the bond that I had with Papa was much stronger than the one I had with her. If Mum was strict, Papa would be lenient, which must have made a difference to any child. If I didn't want to go to nursery, for example, I wouldn't have to because Papa came to the rescue. I would stand by the fridge and cry. 'Come with me, Cassie. I'll take you somewhere nice,' Papa would say lovingly. He would then pick me up, hug me, bundle me into his car and we would speed off to his office together. Instead of going to the nursery, I would spend the day with him at the car-hire firm. It was our little secret.

'Your father was also a natural with you, Cassie. He was so loving to you when you were born and he made us both very happy,' Mum has told me whenever I ask her about Papa. I can still see that she really savours those early memories, but they will never take away the pain of what was to follow.

When I was two years old things at home dramatically changed. Unexpectedly Mum fell pregnant. The unplanned pregnancy created all sorts of problems between her and Papa, mainly because it was such a shock for them both. Papa was always proud of himself for being able to give Mum her first child, but suddenly he felt as if he couldn't cope with another one and buckled under the pressure. 'Any man can make a child, Cassie, but it takes a real man to be a father,' Mum has often said to me when

I've been faced with my own relationship problems. I understand what she means but it must have been tough for Papa at that time because he had a lot on his plate at work and was desperately trying to make a success of his life for the family. I also know myself about the impact an unplanned pregnancy can have on a person. It's a huge shock to the system, but it's the couple's way of handling those difficult feelings and emotions that makes a difference. If one parent can't support the other, then that paves the way for future difficulties.

Anyway, Mum says she thought the birth might have brought them closer over time. She knew it would be incredibly difficult under the circumstances, but, because this upheaval concerned a child, she thought Papa would find it within himself to change. 'Your father never changed,' Mum explains to me when I quiz her about my father. 'I needed a lot more emotional and physical support than he could give me during that time. In the end instead of facing up to the responsibility, he ran away from it,' she says, bowing her head.

Papa's negativity towards bringing a second child into the world took over his life, his mind and everything he did after Mum broke the news to him. His negativity ate him up and he became resentful. In the end he became completely emotionally and physically unsupportive towards her. Sadly, that change in him and his lack of trying to be a father to Ben damaged our cosy family life for good.

Mum remembers the day when she brought Ben home from hospital. Apparently, Papa went straight into the bedroom and slammed the door shut. Mum says she was exhausted, but managed to smile down at me and stroke my hair. 'This is your brother Ben,' she remembers saying. 'Ben loves you, Cassie, just like I do.' She knew I wanted to hold baby Ben straight away, but I wasn't strong enough so she let me kiss his tiny screwed-up face. She says that I immediately felt protective over my adorable little brother, but sadly Papa never witnessed that special moment when his two children first met.

Things then deteriorated considerably between Mum and Papa. By the time Ben had settled in at home, they rarely spoke. Mum says that Papa would spend as much time away from her as he could. A month after Ben was born, he reacted terribly by cheating on Mum. She knew because suddenly other women started knocking at our door at night. Mum would cry softly to herself in her bedroom with the door shut while Papa ushered the women away. She says she remembers me sitting alone in my room and how I seemed to know not to go in and comfort her because nothing would have helped her grief. Mum says that unfortunately the cheating worsened and Papa started staying out all night. His nights away then turned into three-day drinking binges. She knew that I could hear her screaming at Papa in the kitchen when he finally arrived home reeking of wine and women, and she felt terrible knowing how that might impact on Ben and me.

To add fuel to the fire, Papa's business was starting to fail, probably because of his rocky personal life and the drinking. But in the end he just drank his sorrows away, and eventually the business and our family unit completely disintegrated. She didn't have any money for food once he had been gone for three days, but she says he would just laugh it off when she confronted him, waltz out and probably go and find another drink. Mum would end up saving money because she knew things were rocky financially for them. She would hide what she'd saved because she knew if she didn't do that then the money Papa brought in would go elsewhere. Sometimes he would find her savings and spend them on himself.

When Mum explains to me what happened in Spain, I really don't know how she coped. It must have been hard with a newborn child and a two-year-old. She doesn't dwell on it, though, and only talks about it when I ask her. My grandparents still tell me about this difficult time and how it affected Mum. I understand now how this dark period within our family was to affect the rest of my life. You see, Papa had suddenly deserted me. Mum says I'd sit in the living room waiting for him to come home each night to play as we usually did. I must have longed for a hug and kiss from Papa, but, when he started to stay out all night, she says I'd cry when I knew he wasn't coming home. I'd watch the large brown clock tick on the living-room wall and listen for his key in the door, but Papa had gone and he wasn't coming back. Sometimes he would come back after work but then he'd run into the bathroom and get ready to go out. Mum says that I'd cry again in front of him a few times but it didn't make any difference and within an hour of coming home Papa was soon heading off into the night, leaving me sitting there, longing for some time with him.

To this day all Mum cares about are her kids. I know she didn't want us to grow up without a father but she had no choice. Leaving Papa was a brave thing to do, but, when she plucked up the courage and ran away from

Menorca with us, she knew it was for the best. 'We're going to see Granddad and Nan,' Mum told us. She wanted to tell me something that would make me happy that morning and because I was too young to understand the truth she had to be careful with her words.

'Why?' I'd asked her.

'Because we need a holiday, sweetheart,' she'd replied.

'And Papa?'

Mum said she cuddled me in silence, knowing she had no choice but to leave secretly. She tells me she borrowed money from her friends and quickly booked our flights the day before. She then packed up as little as we needed, and when Papa had gone to work she left and bundled us into the back of a taxi. 'The arguments had got so bad and the cheating was much too much for me,' she has since explained. She also said there were days of long silences between them when Papa was hungover and tired or there were more women at the door and then huge rows erupted at the end of it all. Most of all, Mum quite rightly says that she didn't want things to affect her two kids.

When we arrived in England, Mum remembers how upset I was. 'Cassie, wake up, sweetheart. We've landed,' she'd said softly to me as I sat sleeping in the plane seat. Mum says that when I woke up my eyes clouded over with tears because I must've seen fear etched all over her pale, drawn face. She says I knew when I looked up at her that night that Papa wasn't with me any more. To this day she always says that, when things bother me, my teary eyes often give my thoughts and feelings away.

Mum held me tightly as I looked through the tiny plane window into the dark night with tears streaming down my face. She says that I turned around and watched the other passengers bustling past us down the aisle and then I looked down at Ben, who was in the baby bassinette in front of us. 'Where's Papa?' Mum remembers me asking her anxiously. 'Come on,' she said. 'Granddad and Nan are waiting for us in the airport. We're staying with them tonight.' Mum says that she cupped my face, kissed me and wiped away my tears. She then unfastened my seat belt, put my shoes on and helped me stand up. I was still half asleep, but she remembers me looking around the plane, obviously for Papa. Apparently, I reached down to Ben and hugged him, pressing my cheek to his. 'It's me, Ben, I'm still here,' Mum remembers me whispering to him as we left the plane together.

When we began our new life in England that night, the separation from my father probably felt unbearable. Mum knew I was upset and afraid when we landed at Gatwick Airport, but she says that seeing Nan and Granddad in the arrivals area snapped me out of it.

I always think how bad it must have been for Ben. He is two years younger than me but, because our parents' troubles started when he was born, he didn't have any time at all with Papa and, whereas I was old enough to live through it and be fussed over, Ben wasn't given that. He is lovely and warm, though, and through everything we have always been close. Unlike me, Ben is a 'slippers and pipe' man and still loves the security of where he grew up in Kent. Maybe he's like that because he wants to have what Papa didn't – a secure, homely life with a good marriage and a solid, loving relationship.

It was late when we finally arrived on the Isle of

Sheppey and everyone was tired after the long journey. Ben and I were to sleep on the floor in a small spare bedroom and the single bed by the window was for Mum. She knew I'd feel better that night in the unfamiliar bedroom if I slept cuddled up with Ben. And so the three of us settled into my granddad Alf and my nan Rita's house. Nan and Granddad say they squeezed themselves into the bedroom next door and, although space was tight and we only had a few belongings, we grew to love our new home despite my missing my father.

'Is Papa coming to see me soon? Can we go home now? Poor Papa is all alone, Mum,' I'd say to her some mornings when I woke up.

She knew I was often confused and really missed Papa, but she did all she could to help me. 'No, Cassie sweetheart, he's working hard at the moment. He'll come and see you soon. He isn't alone but he loves you.' She knew she couldn't tell me what had really happened between herself and Papa because she didn't want to make me think anything bad about him, plus again, she knew I was too young to understand. Despite how upset I got with Mum at the time, she always acted and continues to act with so much dignity when it comes to Papa and the awful situation between them. She strove hard to love us as much as she could so that without him Ben and I would always feel secure and happy.

A week after we left Menorca, Papa contacted Mum and threatened to steal us back. 'I am coming to get my kids, Karen!' he shouted down the phone.

'But you can't, Pepe. You've been a terrible father – you have neglected us all,' she replied.

Apparently, Mum was beside herself when she got the call from him so she had to go to the police. In the end, they dealt with Papa and subsequently pinned pictures of Ben and I on walls in airports throughout the UK. It's strange to think that Ben and I were under threat of being kidnapped by our own father, but it's true. It must have been frightening for Mum but she fought so hard to keep and protect us.

Once Mum had contacted the police, the threats stopped and she was always willing to let Papa see us. There were no more problems over access to us and Papa didn't ask for anything more than visitation rights – but his visits became less and less frequent once he started seeing his new girlfriend.

One November morning in 1987, Mum sat me down at the kitchen table and told me that Papa wanted to visit. I was four years old and hadn't seen him for more than two years. All I could think about was Christmas and that having Papa around me would be the best present in the world. Mum says she watched a huge smile break out on my face. That day, she explained that, although Papa had acted terribly, she'd agreed to the visit because she knew I missed him. Nana says Mum was very dignified that Christmas and allowed the contact, but then, when he arrived in Sheppey a few weeks later, Papa let us down.

I remember that first trip vividly. 'I'll take you somewhere nice, Cassie,' Papa had promised me as I sat on his knee by the Christmas tree. 'I'm going to be here all week with you. What would you like for Christmas, sweetheart?' he asked.

Mum says I told him I wanted a pony and he promised

me that he would get me one. But Papa never did take me anywhere special that Christmas or get me that pony. He did manage to take Ben and me to the local Happy Eater for lunch, but when he left the next day the hurt and upset I felt only intensified. After that he never bothered to make amends. He continued to act irresponsibly towards me by making empty promises for years to come and so in the end I lost all my trust in him.

For years afterwards I thought that if I couldn't even trust my own father then I wouldn't be able to trust any man. If my father could leave me so isolated and vulnerable then I was sure every other man would do the same. For a long time that's what I thought men did and that it was normal. Papa was the first man to break my heart and that feeling compounded a lot of negativity later on in my life. I think that's perhaps why I tried drugs and mixed with the wrong sort of people when I hit my twenties. Taking drugs was my way of keeping the pain I'd felt as a child in check; it also made me feel like I belonged, even if it was within a completely self-destructive crowd. They made me feel special and wanted, and they concealed the isolation I'd felt for many years beforehand. Luckily, over the years I've managed to conquer my fear of trusting men and have found somewhere much more real to belong. I have also dealt with my anxiety of isolation and become fine about spending time alone. I trust my boyfriend Lee now and feel like I belong with him, so as you can imagine it's such a relief being able to feel all this positivity at last.

After about a year of living in England, we eventually moved to a council house near my grandparents. It was a three-bedroom house with a garden and I felt so lucky having my own pink bedroom. On the day we moved in, I remember getting all my dolls out of their boxes and making them feel at home. It was nice to finally have some space and it really felt like a new beginning. The difficulty was that Mum had to work hard to keep us going. 'I'm working this weekend, Cassie, sorry, sweetheart,' she would tell me most Friday afternoons when I got home from school.

'It's fine, Mum. Don't be sorry, I'll take care of Ben,' I'd say, hugging her. It was tough some weekends if we had a nanny to look after us, but I knew it was harder for Mum because Papa never gave us any money. She didn't pursue Papa for maintenance payments for us because she had brought us to the UK and she knew that there was no point in asking Papa for money. Instead, she would work every hour under the sun and because Ben and I were at school all she wanted was for us to have everything we needed to thrive as children.

I was seven when Mum met and married our stepdad, Patrick. He was always really respectful and kind. I'd warmed to him straight away when Mum came home with him one night in his little red sports car. In fact, Ben and I really adored him and still do. One day, after they'd been seeing one another for a good six months, Ben and I were sitting side by side at the kitchen table when Patrick came in and stood in front of us. 'I wanted to ask you both if I could marry your mum,' he said.

Patrick was tall, blue-eyed and very kind. I smiled up at him and thought, I don't mind if you marry my mum because she is happy now and I like you! Ben and I stood up and went over and hugged Patrick. We didn't need to say anything because we just wanted him to become part of our lives. As well as Patrick, Ben and I were also thrilled to be able to call Patrick's two children, Conor and Megan, our new brother and sister. Patrick always treated us all equally and we became a really close family unit.

Mum and Patrick finally married in Sheerness Church. I was eight years old and I couldn't have been happier that day as I stood watching them exchange vows in my little pink bridesmaid's dress. Mum became Mrs Patrick Sumner and, as she did not want us to have to keep explaining why we had a different surname from her, Ben and I also took her married name. Patrick never officially adopted us, as Papa wouldn't allow it – but, as well as making Mum happy, Patrick also gave us everything we needed throughout the rest of our childhood.

Chapter Two

Bullies and Boys

I WAS 12 YEARS OLD WHEN I SUFFERED AN AWFUL SPATE OF BULLYING. AT THE TIME, I WAS AT SECONDARY SCHOOL AND, WHEN IT GOT REALLY BAD, I WANTED TO HIDE MYSELF AWAY. I felt isolated, detached and afraid because I distrusted the other kids and was unable to confide in anyone at home about my feelings about Papa. However, it was during my first years at St Edwards Primary that elements of distrust, detachment and isolation had set in for different reasons. Those feelings had surfaced because, like I said earlier, I was feeling hurt and neglected by Papa.

On my first day at school, I remember standing at the gates with Mum and watching all the other fathers say goodbye to their children. I remember wishing so hard that morning that it was me. 'Why do they have their papas around them this morning and I don't? It's my first day at school. Shouldn't Papa be here with me?' I'd asked Mum sadly that day.

'You know your father is busy, Cassie. Off you go now and enjoy yourself. I'll collect you later,' she said.

I felt better knowing Mum would be there to see me later, but, as I walked away from her, still it just didn't seem fair. I felt cheated because Papa wasn't there on the day I needed to face a brand-new world. That same feeling of anger continued to plague me every day after that. From the age of four until about six years old, I'd sit alone at the back of the classroom stewing in my own anger. I won't trust a soul, I'd tell myself, as I watched the other kids chatting and playing happily together. I don't want to talk to any of these children or make friends with them. They will only upset me or let me down like Papa has done, I'd think, feeling angry with the world.

My reclusive nature and unwillingness to interact with the other kids carried on even when I went to secondary school, where it affected my academic work. I knew that, if I excelled, I would stand out. Even though I was told that I was naturally bright and was good at art, I didn't want to be placed at the top of the grade list each week. I was determined to remain a 'nobody' and I therefore made sure 'Cassie Sumner' wasn't a name that the other kids ever thought about.

It was at St John Fisher that the bullying began, mainly because I'd started to attract male attention. By the age of 12, my looks were getting noticed and, funnily enough, although the outcome of that welcome attention was negative, that attention gave me my first bit of confidence. I'd never had Papa around to tell me how lovely and special I was, so I lapped up praise from the boys at school. 'You're gorgeous, Cassie. You have the prettiest eyes in the whole school,' I remember them saying to me. I'd always smile back at them and I remember that the compliments they dished out made me feel so good. 'My friend fancies you and wants to be your boyfriend, but I like you too. Have you got a boyfriend, Cassie?' one of the boys might innocently ask at playtimes. 'Can I kiss you after school?' And sure enough when I'd pass through the big black school gates one of them would be waiting there for me, smiling and ready for a kiss. Sometimes I'd let him peck me on the cheek and I'd blush before skipping off happily towards the train station.

That feeling of being attractive and in turn feeling confident enabled me to interact with the other children. My looks had given me a chance to belong and I took it. The feelings of detachment and isolation I'd felt because of Papa started to fade and I finally began to mix in. Being popular with the boys felt nice and I was happy. The boys wanted to talk to me and then, because of that male interest, the girls were keen to talk to me too. Although I was still quite shy, I relished this newfound attention and things seemed to be looking up. After a while I started hanging out with a popular group of girls, which was headed up by a nice girl called Rachel. Petite and pretty, with lovely long straight dark hair, she was also fashionable and had nicer clothes than the rest of us. My parents didn't have a lot of money at that time, so I didn't have expensive things like Rachel had, but all of us got on like a house on fire regardless of what we wore.

One day things suddenly changed and this was dramatic, to say the least. 'I had an argument today with

Jenny,' I remember telling Mum one afternoon when I'd got home from school.

'Don't worry, love, these things happen. Why don't you try to make it up with her tomorrow?' she suggested, as she busied herself over our dinner.

I knew she was right but I also realised things wouldn't be smoothed over so easily with Jenny because she was best friends with a girl who, for the purpose of this book, I'll call Joanne. Joanne was quite pretty and the boys liked her. They knew she was advanced sexually and they would do anything she wanted. Joanne also knew how to assert herself. Her parents would allow her to do anything she wanted – she could drink and smoke, plus she had already messed around with several boys in my class and it was known at the school that her parents didn't mind.

When I also started getting attention from the boys, Joanne couldn't take it. She was jealous. As soon as she heard about the argument with Jenny, they became firm allies and the bullying was under way. She'd say, 'You don't have nice shoes on, Cassie. You look frumpy,' and would then start stamping on my feet. One day we were sitting in the classroom after lunch and Joanne's nasty comments made me feel inadequate. 'You're stupid and you don't know how to kiss,' she snarled and suddenly the boys burst out laughing.

After that it got worse and worse. Most days I'd come home in floods of tears and tell Mum what Joanne was doing and saying to me. Sometimes things would go too far and she would hit me in the playground. Life became unbearable and, between the ages of 13 and 14, I withdrew more and more into my own little world.

Bullies and Boys

Looking back, I now understand that Joanne was insecure. She played this game with me to build up her support network and boost her own confidence – that's what bullies do. Bullying me would give her much more attention and strength, she thought, but in fact it never gives anyone strength – it only shows what a weak person they are.

One day I finally caved in. 'I don't want to go to school today,' I cried to Mum. 'Joanne is bullying me so much at the moment, I can't take it any more!' I said, as I sat at the kitchen table and told Mum everything. I hadn't wanted to tell her much before then because I was afraid, but it had got so bad the week before, that on the Monday I didn't even want to go to school.

'Right!' she snapped. 'I'm going in with you this morning, Cassie. Go upstairs, get your things and then sit and wait for me in the car.'

Minutes later, Mum had emerged from the house with her coat on. She looked like she was going to a business meeting and later I found out that she'd already called the school and was going to meet the headmistress. I remember sitting nervously in the school common room: I knew Mum was in with the headmistress, telling her all about Joanne.

That morning I felt such fear because of what the other kids would think of me for telling on her. Some of them liked Joanne and I thought they would hate me now for speaking to Mum. When one of the teachers finally appeared, she told us that Joanne had been expelled. My heart sank and I was scared because the other kids would know from seeing Mum that she'd been expelled because of me.

'It's fine, Cassie,' said one of the other girls, smiling. She'd come up to me and sat down next to me. 'You did the right thing by telling your mum. Joanne deserved it. She's a bully and she needs to learn,' she said, comforting me.

I felt such relief and smiled back at her. I knew I wasn't the only one who was sick of Joanne, but I was surprised to learn that I actually had support from the other kids. 'Well done, Cassie,' they all said, after they saw how worried I looked. Jenny even came over and hugged me and I felt relief, thinking that the bullying was finally over, though that turned out to be far from the case.

The next week, the bullying intensified and, because it was outside the school's control, it got much worse. Joanne also lived on the Isle of Sheppey and, when she started at another school, she would simply meet me off the train every day with her cousin. She couldn't forget me because I was the one who'd actually got her expelled.

Whenever I travelled home from school each day on the train, I would feel terror; when the train pulled into the station I'd normally start to panic. Often I'd have to move my face away from the train window in case they saw me. I'd spot the two bullies standing grinning together on the platform. When the train stopped, my heart would beat harder and faster, and my hands always felt clammy. I'd often change carriages and would take a deep breath and then walk swiftly through one carriage and into the adjoining one. Unfortunately, the bullies normally spotted me when I opened the train door and the sight of them always made me freeze with fear. 'We've been waiting for you, Sumner!' Joanne would shout, as she ran towards me.

Normally I tried to hide among the other passengers

crossing the platform, but usually Joanne had already worked her way through the huge throng of people and would be blocking my path. Wild-eyed, she'd stare at me, while her cousin would grab my schoolbag. Then, using all her force, Joanne would push me over. I'd be lying on the concrete, my voice trapped inside me and my head pounding from the fall, but I knew that, if I tried to get up, I'd be hurt again. Sometimes I'd feel a hand across my face and pain would sear through my head. 'Leave me alone, give me back my schoolbag!' I'd murmur, as my body trembled.

Just as the day before, whatever I said to those two girls never made any difference. The next day I knew they'd be waiting for me on the platform again. I dreaded that ten-minute journey on the train home from school. Sometimes I'd feel relief when the girls weren't waiting on the platform but that only meant that they would be there the next day. For months, Joanne and her cousin continued those platform rampages.

Despite the fact that she would slap and kick me, I never hit Joanne back. Often I'd come home, run up to my room and cry my eyes out. Sometimes I felt so distraught that I'd throw up. It's horrific for a child at that age because you feel helpless. I felt helpless because I'd told Mum and, because I'd confided in her, the bullying had got worse. I thought that, if I told anyone this time around what was going on, something awful would happen to me.

'I really can't go into town with you,' I'd say to my friends most Saturday mornings when they called me. 'I just can't – I have things to do.' And, although I desperately wanted to spend time with them, shopping and having coffee, I could never tell them why I had to stay in. Like I could never tell Mum again. I never wanted to be set upon again as I had been the last time I'd ventured into town. You see, Joanne would always be at the same bus stop in the town centre. It was her hangout point and all the boys would surround her whenever she was there. The day I'd gone into town and had walked past the bus stop, I saw them all huddled together, gossiping and laughing. I prayed she hadn't seen me.

'You're a slapper and a slag, Sumner. We're going to get you!' they all shouted and then they started to run towards me.

I turned around quickly and fled. I ran as fast as I could towards the train station because I didn't want to be hit. Luckily they didn't catch up with me, but I knew I could never go into town again in case Joanne did catch me.

Fortunately, the bullying gradually fizzled out. I assume Joanne must have become bored of it. But it stopped properly when the older girls at my school started to stick up for me and she then backed off completely. By that time, I'd met my best friend Nicola O'Connell, who was a year older than me. Joanne knew she had no chance with the other girls around me all the time. Funnily enough, just as Nicola and her friends had become deterrents from Joanne's bullying, they also injected some much-needed fun into my life.

I was 14 when Nicola introduced me to the wonderful world of clubbing. Clubbing completely distracted me from anything negative that was happening around me. It was amazing fun and I felt all grown up whenever I went out. I felt part of something and part of a fun-loving and vibrant crowd. 'Come out with us tonight, Cassie!' Nicola would say to me every Saturday afternoon and I'd spend the next few hours stressing about what to wear and planning what to tell Mum. Because of my age, I knew Mum would never have allowed me to go out to a nightclub, but I always found a way of keeping my nights out with Nicola and her sisters a secret. 'I'm staying with Nicola tonight, Mum,' I'd explain, knowing full well that upstairs in my bedroom my bag was packed with mini skirts, crop tops and make-up, ready for the big night ahead. Although she never questioned or doubted me, Mum was right to be strict with me. She wasn't stupid and knew full well that I was attracting attention from boys at school, but somehow I managed to get away with the 'Nicola' story or at least for a while.

Regardless of Mum's rules, I knew clubbing had given me a release and made me feel happy, so I stuck with it no matter what. The first night we went out I'd bought a slinky bronze, sparkly mini dress. I felt so cool when I entered our favourite haunt 'Woodys', but it was the male attention I got when I started clubbing that made me feel really happy and confident. Everything that had happened before, with either Papa or the bullies, had knocked me for six, but, whenever I was at Woodys with Nicola and we were having fun, I was always able to forget about my past and feel like I belonged somewhere. Because I'd been quite shy at school, I think I was still impressionable. I'd always watch other older girls and men around me at Woodys and I wanted to be like them. I needed to show everyone that I was confident and invincible, and just like they were.

That first night I remember feeling a release inside me as I stood in the middle of the club. I felt fantastic as I stood there, like a grown-up, sipping my cocktail. 'This is amazing,' I told Nicola. I felt so alive as I looked around the small room flooded with coloured lights and thumping music. There were three small dance floors and a DJ booth in the middle. Straight away I noticed that there were older boys everywhere and, because they were so friendly and welcoming to me on that first night out, I felt really special and wanted. Funnily enough, when I was later to start clubbing on the London scene, it was that same feeling of joy, a sense of freedom and belonging that also helped me forget my troubles during that difficult period.

It was on one of those heady Saturday nights that I met my first boyfriend – I'll call him Dan, not his real name. I was only 15 at the time, but I fell for him simply because he was a few years older. He made me feel like he would protect and care for me, just as Papa must have done when I was a baby. All the same feelings of warmth and happiness that I had when Papa had visited me from Spain flooded back and I felt happy because the gap in my life was finally filled. Although we weren't together for a long period, I would spend time with Dan dancing in the club and then we would head back to his place in Sheppey. I would have to lie more to Mum, though, when I saw him because I knew she would never approve of his age.

Sadly, although our age gap brought us together, it ended our brief relationship and I even fell out with Nicola because of it. 'Your mum has called me, Cassie. I can't lie for you any more,' I remember Nicola shouting down the phone one day when I was at Dan's.

That day I was lying in his bed when my mobile phone woke us up. I looked at the time on the phone: it was 11am. 'What do you mean, Nic?' I asked sleepily. 'What's wrong?'

'Your mum called my house to ask if you and I wanted to have lunch at yours today and I had to tell her the truth,' she replied.

I froze. 'What did she say?' I asked.

'They asked where Dan lived and she then said that they are coming to get you now,' she replied.

I hung up and jumped out of the bed; I needed to get dressed quickly and out of the door. 'What's wrong, Cas? Where are you going?' Dan asked, still half asleep.

'My parents are coming – I have to go! I don't want them to see you.'

Dan went silent. He was confused because, although he knew something was wrong, he didn't understand why so much drama was unfolding in his bedroom that Sunday morning. I hadn't even put my top on when the doorbell went. 'It's them, I have to go,' I said anxiously, and ran downstairs and opened the front door.

Mum and Patrick were standing in front of me, their faces stern. 'Why have you been lying to us, Cassie? You need to come home with us now to explain yourself!' Mum said angrily.

I started to walk out of the house when I felt Dan's hand on my shoulder. Patrick stepped forward and the two of them argued. I can't remember exactly what was said because I was crying so much, but Patrick told Dan to leave me alone and that he was taking me home. My parents were furious, but I was more than distraught. Not only had I lost another man, but also it felt as if Mum didn't want me to be happy. I thought I was in love with Dan, just as I had loved Papa, but felt that she had driven us apart. That day I hated Mum so much and I hated Papa just as much for not being there to comfort me. I also fell out with Nicola because she was cross with me for having to lie to Mum. Everyone was angry with me and by the evening my emotions were starting to overwhelm me.

That night I knew I had to do something. I needed Mum to understand me and for Papa to come and be with me. I'd found a real happiness again, yet it felt as if it was being taken away from me and that seemed to have been the pattern in my life. Papa and the bullies had taken away my happiness and now Mum had, too – or so it seemed to me. I went into the bathroom and opened the cabinet above the sink. I remember reaching for the bottle of paracetamol and swallowing as many pills as I could. At the time I was thinking in dismay, I don't want to die – for once I just want someone to care about me and what I feel; I just want someone to allow me to feel happy for once.

I really felt as if I didn't have anyone to turn to and I wanted the shouting to stop. I was also hurt that Dan hadn't bothered to fight for me that day. In fact, he didn't even say goodbye or call later. That night, I took an overdose and, when Mum and Patrick found me in the bathroom, they rushed me to hospital to get my stomach pumped. Fortunately, I hadn't taken enough pills to cause any real harm, but the overdose made everyone in my family understand how I was really feeling. They knew that the underlying reason for my taking an overdose was a cumulation of negative feelings brought on by the bullying I had suffered, my father leaving and the feeling that a man I thought had cared about me perhaps didn't. I'd never cried openly to Mum about Papa or told her how much it hurt that Papa had neglected me, so taking the pills that night actually created a deeper sense of caring between Mum and I. We didn't discuss it after that, but she knew how I felt and that was what mattered more to me. Despite Mum's understanding of me and my feelings, the real difficulty for me was that the confused and negative feelings I had about Papa were getting stronger. I knew they would become more pertinent to my life as I strove to find love and trust other men, that it was only a matter of time before I would finally be strong enough to confront him.

Chapter Three

A Bolt From Bluewater

Dear Papa,

I hope you're well.

We haven't spoken in a long time so I'm not even sure if you're still at this address.

I wanted to get in touch because I need to let you know how I feel. I also think it's time for me to try and finally understand you.

The distance between you and I over the years has affected and hurt me and I've often wished that you were there for me. Not only has it been difficult without you around, but also it upset me when you used to make promises to me and never keep them.

I'm eighteen now and fairly happy with my life, but I've always felt there was something missing and unresolved in my life. I know now that those negative feelings centre on you, your absence and your empty promises.

Please call if you want to because it would mean so much to me if we could finally talk through things together as adults and iron things out.

With love

Cassie x

I was 18 when I felt strong enough to write to Papa. I remember that when I signed my name at the end of the letter I could barely read the words on the page because my eyes had filled with tears. I folded the letter carefully and put it in the envelope but as I wrote Papa's old address across the front I remember identifying with the pain and confusion I'd felt through the years. When I turned away from the postbox, I remember feeling a great release inside me; and the pain started to subside. My tears stopped and I'd smiled to myself because just letting Papa know that he'd hurt me was a big step. I knew that just writing the letter would make me stronger because I'd finally taken control of the situation and I knew that that control would help me move on. I also wanted the letter to make Papa think about being a better father to his other two kids than he had been to me.

I knew the letter would take a few days to get to Spain. It was Wednesday when I'd sent it, so I remember thinking Papa would call at the weekend when it had arrived at his place. But the weekend came and went, and I heard nothing. I remember the next week was particularly tough. Every time my mobile rang and 'withheld number' popped up, I hoped it might be Papa; every time the phone would ring at home, my heart would beat faster and I'd pray it was him. But the days just came and went and he didn't ever write back or call me. What doesn't kill you, Cassie, can only make you stronger, I remember telling myself over and over during those nights when I'd lie in bed thinking about Papa and imagining him opening my letter.

The next weekend he finally rang. 'Your father called today, Cassie,' I remember Mum saying anxiously. 'He told me that you wrote to him but he was angry with me about what you wrote.'

Papa had finally made contact, but he didn't call *me*. He'd called Mum and told her that he didn't want to talk to me. His response, or lack of it, hurt a lot but at least I'd got some sort of answer.

'He said that I've done a bad job bringing you up because you're rude to have written a letter like that. You need to move on, sweetheart, because your father obviously has,' she said. She knew it was important for me to get some sort of resolution, but she also knew I was talking to a brick wall. 'Don't worry, sweetheart,' she said lovingly. 'Your father does love you but he may never face up to the mistakes he made. You need to start getting on with your life now. Your father has a new family now and so do you. Patrick and I love and care about you so much, Cassie. You really need to try to let go of the past.'

At the time, of course, I was upset but I never cried in front of Mum. I knew she meant well and she was supportive, but I still felt angry that Papa had messed my life up and not bothered to make amends. In my mind, he refused to take responsibility for his recklessness. But then I also knew that day that I needed to forget him and let go, otherwise my feelings would carry on eating away at me. Yes, I felt insecure and unloved, and I also felt cheated out of something everyone else had in their lives but it was obvious that Papa wasn't ever going to change. By now Papa had two other children, both boys – Enrique and Alex – and I don't know if this affected how he felt about Ben and I but that day I decided that the easiest way for me to move on was to try to forget. And that's exactly what I did. The only problem was that, later on in my life, when I entered the modelling world and tried hard to find love and security elsewhere, it came in the form of unsuitable people, partying and drugs. I'd felt isolated from Papa as a child and so, as I grew up, I became quite desperate to feel wanted and to belong somewhere I'd assumed was much more real and more special.

After that night, every time a thought of Papa came into my mind I'd ignore it or quickly think of something else that was nice. I cut everything to do with Papa out of my life. Thoughts, feelings and memories were all put in a box and the lid firmly shut. Papa was now history. Getting him back and having some understanding of it all just wasn't going to happen. I took comfort in knowing that writing to Papa only proved I was growing stronger inside and that now I could actually confront things when I really wanted to. I'd finally made a new start. Strangely enough, at the same time my life changed regardless of Papa, the letter and the new path I'd decided to take without him.

Over the years I'd always heard people tell Mum that I should be a model. Mum's friends would look at me and tell her that I was pretty. 'You should send your Cassie up to that model agency,' her best friend Sally would often say when they were sitting, chatting away together in the kitchen on Sunday afternoons. As soon as I'd hear my name mentioned downstairs, I would always creep to the top of the staircase and listen. 'Cassie is so pretty, Karen. She could really make something of herself. Her eyes have something in their own right: they are so expressive when she looks at you and everyone always comments on them,' Sally would say.

Mum would quickly change the subject, but that was what always happened when the modelling topic came up in conversation at home.

It was when I overheard Mum and Sally that I'd also remember a man who used to get the train with me to school every day. He would always say to me, 'You'll be a model when you are older, trust me!' and I always felt like telling Mum that, too. But, as you can guess, modelling wasn't something she ever wanted me to do. 'You both need to study hard at school and get through your exams – getting into college and doing a degree is the only way forward in life. That final piece of paper will get you your dream job and make sure you have a good prosperous future,' she'd always tell Ben and me harshly. Quite rightly, she drummed it into our heads that a decent education would give us all we wanted in life. For Mum, one issue was that she had really struggled financially when she left Papa in Menorca. She knew full well that, if she had had a degree, things would have been a lot easier for all of us when we arrived in the UK. But the other reason why Mum was reluctant to discuss the modelling was that she had worked herself to the bone to make sure our home life continued to support our education. She made sure we had decent uniforms, books and were able to go on school trips just like all the other kids. For this reason, I knew that I owed it to her to make a success of myself at school and at college. Up until then I'd done her proud at school despite the real hopes that lay buried inside me.

Most nights in my teens, I'd think about my hopes of becoming a model. I'd love to be a top model like Kate

Moss, I'd often think when I lay in bed at night. I'd lie awake dreaming about catwalks, photo shoots and travelling around the world, mixing with the rich and famous and having an amazingly luxurious lifestyle. The whole modelling industry really intrigued me. Sometimes when I woke up in the morning and got ready for school I'd still be daydreaming; I'd pout and pose in the bathroom mirror and wonder which way I should hold and turn my head so that I'd look the best on camera. Then, on the way to the train station, I'd often stop off at the local newsagents to buy fashion magazines like *Elle* and *Vogue* just to see what top models really looked like.

The other problem I knew I had at that time was that I still wasn't very confident. Although everyone told me I had good looks and I knew that I was pretty, I didn't feel good about my figure: I was pear-shaped and so I thought I might get rejected if I tried modelling. I certainly didn't want to look a fool if I failed. So, despite my hopes and daydreams, it was much easier for me to stick with what I was already doing and what I knew I was good at; it was safer and easier that way. I'd already won a place at Minster College in Sheppey to study Law and so everything was in place and ready to go as far as my education was concerned. My career was set in stone and the idea of modelling becoming a reality was further away than ever – until Bluewater.

I was out shopping with Mum at the Bluewater shopping complex in Kent when fate intervened in my life. At the time, I was 18 and had just written to Papa. Out of nowhere, a woman approached me as we were looking at the make-up section in Boots. 'Have you ever modelled?' she asked.

I remember looking at her and thinking how pretty she was. 'What do you mean?' I replied.

'I mean, would you be interested in trying out to be a model? There is definitely something really unique and special about you,' she said, her round brown eyes focused sharply on mine. The woman's intense gaze wandered over my face and then down over my body.

I smiled at her, wide-eyed with excitement, because I just couldn't believe what I was hearing. The woman seemed like a normal professional woman and straight away I felt comfortable with her. When someone approaches you in the street from nowhere, it can sometimes be daunting, but this woman was different. I remember feeling relaxed and calm with her, as if I had known her for years. 'I'm just a student,' I'd told her that day, as I glanced at Mum, who was busying herself at a nearby counter. 'I'm going to study Law so I don't know anything about modelling at all.'

The woman quickly explained to me that she was a model agent and that she was running a small, but new model agency in London. My heart was pounding as she explained, 'It's unusual for me to see decent-looking girls out on the street any more. I had to come and speak to you for that reason. I know it must be a shock, but sometimes in life things happen for a reason. It is fate that I spotted you today. Will you have a think about coming to see me and doing some test shots?'

Because of the words she had used, I knew that the woman and I were on exactly the same wavelength. I can't show Mum I'm excited. Just take the woman's card and walk away, I thought. I was so afraid Mum wouldn't have approved if I showed any interest, so, when the woman mentioned the test shoot, I politely took her card and we said our goodbyes. Mum was already halfway down the escalators when I looked back and waved the woman goodbye. She smiled back at me warmly and deep down I knew that I would see her again and that she had been right about 'fate'. I buried the business card in my pocket and quickly followed Mum down the escalators.

Together, we walked in silence towards where our car was parked and we stayed like that all the way home. Despite Mum's feelings on the matter and the painful silence between us, I couldn't wait to get home and tell my boyfriend Damian, who was just as excited when I told him what had happened. 'I knew it, Cassie!' I remember him saying. 'I knew my beautiful girl had something special about her. I knew you had amazing eyes. I'll help you in whatever way you need. Where and when do we start?' he asked. He was bursting with happiness for me as I sat and told him every single detail about the Bluewater meeting. But that was Damian – he was always so adorable, kind and supportive.

I'd met Damian when I was 17 and he was my first love. He was the type of guy that everyone in our social set fancied and, like a lot of other girls I knew, I was attracted to him the first time I saw him at Woody's. 'I haven't seen you in here before,' he'd said that first time we met on the dance floor at the club. He was tanned and had fair, sun-kissed hair and handsome, chiselled features. I could see that he was really fit and toned because his arm muscles were bulging through the sleeves of his thin white T-shirt. He smiled at me and I melted. 'I'm Damian,' he continued. 'Who do I have the pleasure of talking to?'

My eyes lit up but I could hardly get my words out. I stopped dancing and he took my hand and pulled me towards the crowded bar.

That night we clicked straight away. The difficulty was that, although we really fancied each other, Damian already had a serious girlfriend. I would never try to split a couple up, but, as I said before about the modelling, I have always been a believer in fate and I don't tend to force things to happen in my life. With Damian I knew that we would eventually be together and, once again, fate played its hand. After that first night at Woody's, I would sometimes spot him out shopping with his girlfriend in Sheppey or we would see one another when we were clubbing at Woody's. Each time I saw him, though, I grew fonder of him. Sometimes we chatted and other times Damian would throw a huge smile my way and my heart would skip a beat. I knew it was only a matter of time.

It was when I started to date a friend of ours that we began to feel more for one another. I'd just started seeing a local guy called Matt Parsons, but it was only a bit of fun. 'How's it going with Matt?' Damian asked me one night when we were all out at Woodys. 'Are you in love?'

'It's nothing serious. Unfortunately you were taken when he asked me out!' I replied, smiling up at him.

Damian grinned at me knowingly and it was clear that he still liked me. That particular evening we ended up chatting all night at the bar, ignoring everyone and anyone around us. The spark between us felt unreal and so it didn't surprise me when Damian finally asked me for my number a few weeks later after he'd told me that he'd split with his girlfriend. 'I've split up with Jodie,' he said slowly one night.

'Why? Oh I am sorry,' I replied.

'No, don't be, it was the right thing. We weren't meant to be and we are both still friends. It's fine,' he explained.

I didn't want to pry and I felt upset for him, but underneath I couldn't contain my happiness. The timing was perfect because Damian was free and I wasn't getting along with Matt.

It wasn't a great way of getting together but, from that point on, nothing could have separated us. There was way too much chemistry between us. Matt hadn't noticed me all that night anyway and was busy chatting to some of his mates in a corner at the club. That was usual for him but I wasn't bothered because I knew we were going nowhere. I quickly wrote my number on an empty cigarette packet and that was it; after that Damian and I became an item. I knew immediately that here at last was a man I could trust and let in. I'd written to Papa by that time and consequently felt stronger as a person. I was ready to commit my feelings to a man and wanted to at least try to love someone.

Damian was an honest person through and through so I knew I could try to open up with him. He grew to know everything about me: how Papa had hurt me, how I'd been bullied at school. It was a relief to be able to talk through things with another man and to be able to lean on him. During my time with Damian, I felt supported and secure and I also discovered real sex with him. I really loved the fact that through sex I could actually show my feelings towards someone, that sex wasn't just an act of enjoyment but a means of expression too.

On the day of Bluewater, Damian really showed me his

true colours. 'You're going to be a top model. My Cassie's going to be a top model!' I remember him saying over and over as he wrapped his arms around my waist and danced me around the bedroom. I don't know what Mum must have thought downstairs, but I was enjoying every minute of his excitement for me. 'I love you for supporting me. I can't do this without you,' I said, kissing his face as we fooled around together like a couple of kids.

I had been given the chance to follow a dream, the chance to build on my hopes and Damian was the one who made me make that journey. I felt confident about it first because someone in the industry had said I had something, but it was Damian who made sure that glimmer of confidence was transferred into action.

That night I also needed to discuss other issues with him that I thought might affect 'us' if I modelled. After the initial buzz of excitement we had calmed down and I'd started to think ahead. 'Will you mind seeing me in photographs wearing a bikini?' I asked him seriously that night. 'It's important to me that we discuss this now. I just need to be sure you'll be happy too if I do this.' What I know now is that, quite rightly, most men find it hard to see their girlfriends semi-naked in photographs, or in photographs at all. Models often lose their partners because of this and I didn't want to lose him at all.

'Cassie, I trust you and just want you to be happy. I wouldn't ever stop you from living your dream and I'll be proud seeing my girl in a magazine or newspaper. You've got something special and you should get out there and show it off,' he replied.

I knew Damian wouldn't become jealous or feel

threatened if I was a success, but we were right to talk about that topic before I committed myself and made a start.

'What if I fail?' I asked him.

'You won't, though, and, if you do, you have nothing to lose,' he replied.

That night we talked and talked about what to do and what things might happen, but we decided that I should at least try out the Bluewater woman's agency. If I didn't photograph well, then I still had my Law degree to do anyway. I knew that with Damian's support behind me I had nothing to lose.

It was over a week later when I decided to call Cameo Models. I chose a Monday morning because everyone was out at home, plus I think people are always better to chat to after the weekend. When the woman answered the phone, she seemed rushed and edgy. I felt uncomfortable and wanted to put the phone down because my nerves and apprehension got the better of me. I suddenly wanted to forget everything. 'It's Cassie, the girl you met at Bluewater last week. Remember the girl in Boots?' I'd said quietly on the phone.

As soon as I reminded her who I was she warmed to me straight away and her tone quickly changed. 'Oh fantastic! It's great you called. Can you come up on Monday at 2pm and do your test shoot? Just come as you are, darling. Everything will be done for you when you get here. If you can just call my assistant during the week for the address,' she explained and put the phone down.

I didn't have time to answer her or ask her any questions, but it didn't matter because all I could think about was the four days I had to prepare myself.

From that moment on, all I could think about was how I needed to look my best. I thought about my hair, nails, clothes and going to the gym. I had a lot of work to do, but the excitement within me was so strong nothing seemed to faze me as I started to prepare myself rigorously. I didn't know the first thing about what a model needed to do for a test shoot so I rushed down to the newsagents and bought all the tabloids. I flicked through pages of the *Sun* and the *Daily Star*. The girls on Page 3 all looked so confident and stunning I didn't know if I could pull it off. 'Can I look like they do, Damian?' I remember asking him that evening as I sat on the bed with the day's papers spread out in front of us.

'Listen, Cas, just do your best. Everyone knows you have what it takes. The agent wouldn't have approached you if you didn't look like these girls.' Damian assured me again that I could make it work and that he would be there to help me.

That night I also practised posing in the mirror in the bathroom with one of the papers next to me. Damian sat on the floor by the bath and smiled up at me, telling me I looked more beautiful than ever.

On the day of the shoot I was prepared and ready. I was toned and fit from the gym, my hair was sleek and glossy and my nails natural yet perfect. I wasn't actually nervous at all. I woke up that Friday morning next to Damian feeling calm and full of hope. He hugged and kissed me when I said goodbye, smiling up from the covers as he said, 'You look stunning, Cassie. You will do so well today, I know it!' And I felt stronger than ever.

That day I caught the midday train from Sheppey to

London. The shoot was in two hours. I've got plenty of time, I told myself, feeling relaxed and happy. The trouble was that I'd spent so much time thinking about how I looked and felt that I'd totally forgotten that I needed to spend time planning my journey properly. I'd never been to London before so wasn't familiar with the traffic and the transport system. When the train pulled into Charing Cross station, I decided to hop on a bus because I knew buses were cheaper. I checked the map at the bus stop, which showed there was a stop right near to where the model agency was. I jumped on happily and sat at the back of the bus and relaxed.

What I hadn't anticipated was the heavy London traffic and the weather! It was raining hard when my bus stop finally came up. The bus had taken double the amount of time because of the traffic jams and when I started to walk the rain was getting everywhere. Five minutes into the ten-minute walk and my feet were sodden, my hair frizzy and my make-up running down my face in streaks. I was so upset with myself because all the work I had done had gone to pot just because I hadn't planned my route or thought about timings and the weather. I ended up arriving a few minutes late for the shoot, but I knew that I looked a proper state and was in tears by the time I greeted the woman. You only live and learn. I hadn't thought for one minute that because I was a model there would be make-up artists and stylists at hand!

'Don't worry, love,' the woman said kindly. 'My make-up artist will sort you out. It doesn't matter how you look today because we're only doing a test shoot. If it were a formal job, then you'd have to be more careful about timings and weather. Just remember that for the future.' I could tell that she was only giving me good advice but I will always remember what she said next. 'I was a model myself, Cassie, so I know the ropes. I understand what you're going through and how you're feeling, but today you need to relax and just enjoy yourself. If you've got natural beauty and confidence, then you're always going to be a winner in this game. Don't feel threatened or intimidated by anyone else out there. The most important thing for you to do when you step into this industry is to keep your head down, keep your dream at the front of your mind and just be yourself.'

It was great advice, but sadly this was the only really good piece of advice I was ever given from an agent when I started out as a model and that is what still pains me.

As soon as I sat down in the make-up chair, the tension disappeared completely. I stared at my naked face in the huge mirror surrounded by big bright lights. This is it, I thought. Cassie, you're a model! I thought over and over as the make-up girl applied layers of foundation, mascara and lipstick. She spent an hour dusting, painting and dabbing my face with colours and gloss, and in the end I have to say the final product looked amazing. I realised I was in my element because I love being pampered anyway, but it was what the make-up girl had created that made me see the beauty I really had. Immediately the confidence I'd felt with Damian in the bathroom at home resurfaced and I knew that I had what it took to be a good model.

'Go and find something sexy in the box behind you,' I remember the woman saying. 'Choose whatever you think suits you and then we can start the shoot.'

So I stripped down to my underwear behind a screen and chose a baby-pink two-piece. I couldn't believe how I was feeling and looking when I stared back at my body and face in the full-length mirror. I thought of Papa and the bullies, and I smiled to myself. If only they could all see me now! Papa would be so proud and Joanne so jealous. I look a million dollars and I know now that I do have something special, I thought. Immediately I wanted to show off what I had to the photographer, but also to show the world that Cassie Sumner was indeed a confident and beautiful woman!

'Are you ready?' shouted the photographer.

Thoughts of Papa and the bullies quickly disappeared as I walked happily into the studio. I've got to focus on the here and now, the past is the past now and I need to think about 'me', I told myself and began to concentrate on the job at hand. The photographer was waiting in front of two huge white backdrops and asked me to stand hands on hips, facing him full on. I didn't even hesitate. Straight away, the huge lights shone on my skin: it felt warm and comforting. He didn't even need to tell me what to do after that – I seemed to know naturally when to move, how to move and what to do for him. Sometimes I smiled, sometimes I pouted. It was all so easy and fun as I looked sexily into the lens. Instinctively I knew what to do. It was a piece of cake and I was right to feel so positive. When I saw the shots I was thrilled.

'These are really sexy,' beamed the photographer. 'I'm really pleased with you, Cassie. It's rare to get such good-quality test shots as these. This is a great start.'

When I looked at my shots, just as I had seen in the

mirror beforehand, I saw a stunning, sexy confident woman instead of a scared and confused little girl. The girl from Sheppey who'd lost her father and been bullied was a million miles away. For me, doing the modelling shoot that day was an escape and I was so proud of myself for making it happen. Looking back, modelling did make me into a different person straight away. It felt right when I glanced at myself in the mirror in the studio, but then, after the shoot, the test shots proved to me that my new career path was the right one.

That evening I was so excited when I caught the train home from Charing Cross that when I arrived in Sheppey I ran home from the station and straight into the house to find Damian waiting for me. He was upstairs in the bedroom watching TV. I jumped on to the bed and hugged him, then pulled out my test shots from my handbag.

'Just as I'd imagined, these are mind-blowing, Cassie!' he said happily. Damian obviously loved them and hugged me closely.

I looked like a proper model and felt so proud that, on my own, I'd taken the first real step and created something truly amazing for myself.

Chapter Four

Body Beautiful

ALTHOUGH MY TEST SHOTS LOOKED FABULOUS, I WASN'T
TOTALLY HAPPY WITH MY FIGURE. In the flesh I still felt I
looked pear-shaped and assumed that I could look much
better with bigger boobs. I also thought that, if I wanted
to cut it as a glamour model, I would need to look 100 per
cent perfect. Because I was focusing all my attention on
my test shots and on how my figure looked, I began to
remember the nasty remarks that I used to hear at school
about my breasts. 'Touching Cassie's boobs must feel like
running your hands over a plank of wood!' the boys
would say, as they sniggered at the back of the classroom.
They would always get their window of opportunity
whenever the teacher left the room and I'd bow my head
so they couldn't see my tears.

I remember that I was sitting in a Maths lesson when the
jibes about my small boobs first started. At the time, I was

14 and it felt as if I was getting a double dose of nastiness because I'd just got over the awful bullying period with Joanne. This new and unexpected spate of cruelty about my shape just wasn't helping matters because my confidence was suffering yet again. Try to ignore them, stay strong, I'd tell myself as I sat at my desk. They are just like Joanne; they are weak and insecure, I'd think. But the remarks often worsened at home time when I'd be standing in front of my locker. 'This is what it feels like when you touch Cassie's chest,' one of the boys would shriek and then he'd run his hands down the corridor wall. 'It feels hard and flat. Yuck!' he'd exclaim and all the others would laugh hysterically. It felt worse during these corridor instances because I was sure everyone was staring at me as they passed by.

And so mocking my figure soon became a regular event for the boys and, although I could normally predict when it was coming, it continued to shock, upset and embarrass me every time it happened. I thought they used to like the way I looked, I'd think, confused, each time it happened. Instead of the boys telling me I was pretty, like they used to, now the focus had turned to my flat chest. I'll never be attractive now and have a nice figure like the other girls, I'd think to myself in despair. My girlfriends were really supportive, though, and would say 'You're so pretty, Cassie. It doesn't matter about your shape anyway. Just ignore it. Yours will grow in their own time!' and I would feel slightly better, but never satisfied inside.

'Can I at least buy a Wonderbra? Can we go out and get one today?' I'd beg Mum most weekends.

'No, Cassie, you aren't ready yet. Why don't we wait

another year, sweetheart, and then I'll take you up to London and we'll find something nice together. It would be a waste of money right now,' she would say.

And with that, I'd skulk off up to my bedroom.

As I went through my late teens, worries about my figure never went away. At 18, I was still pear-shaped and then, after the modelling shoot, it became more pressing for me to change it. I'd first broached the subject of surgery with Damian, who of course loved the way I was naturally. 'Your figure is lovely the way it is,' he would tell me over and over when I brought up the topic of having a boob job. 'Just look at yourself in the photographs you did at the agency! I wouldn't change anything about your body if I were you, Cassie. You're a natural looker.'

He was right about the photographs because my modelling shots did look fantastic; I did look good with my natural shape. But 'good' wasn't good enough in the modelling world and, after all, those shots were only pictures.

One day I decided to tell Mum what I wanted to do. I knew she wouldn't approve, but I felt that, if I was going to take such an important step, I owed it to her to tell the truth. 'I'm getting a loan out, Mum, and I'm going to have a boob job next month,' I suddenly told her one morning as she was leaving for work. I'd considered not telling her about the loan I was thinking of getting, but I really wanted her approval and support. I'd decided to be upfront about my modelling dreams but, at that point when I brought up the question of surgery, we still hadn't discussed modelling as a full-time career.

'But, Cassie, you look beautiful the way you are,

sweetheart. Everyone says so to Patrick and I all the time. Let's talk about it tonight when I get home from work,' she replied. And with that she headed off to work.

I felt better that I'd told Mum and she didn't raise the topic again when she got home that night so I just left it. She knows how stubborn I am when I set my mind on something. Anyway, I'd already submitted my paperwork for the loan to the bank – the operation was going to set me back over £3,000 – and so nothing was stopping me. As soon as I got the OK from the bank, I booked the consultation. I'd already started to look on the Internet for information about implants because I wanted to do my homework – I'd heard so many surgical horror stories and didn't want to make a mistake. Silicone implants had been recommended to me and I decided that an E cup was the largest I wanted to go. I'd always felt that my boobs were rather out of proportion with my otherwise pear-shaped figure so I hoped that, by going to a size E, I would even things up a bit!

Everything went well when I went for my consultation at the Harley Street clinic. As soon as I met the surgeon, I knew I trusted him, so I didn't waste any time. I paid my deposit and booked the operation day. It was all so quick and easy, and, up until the day of the operation, I was completely relaxed and excited about it. Mum knew that I was going ahead with it because Damian had told her, and he also said he'd be there for me if I needed him.

On the day of the operation, Damian drove me up to the hospital in North London where I was to have the operation. 'This is important to you, Cassie. I'm here for you now and will be there for you when it's over. You've nothing to worry about,' he said, stretching his hand over mine as we sat in the car together outside the hospital.

Nerves had started to get the better of me by that point and Damian had noticed my pale face when he stopped the car. He knew me inside out and that helped so much. He always supported everything I did and again this was another situation where he was there for me. Looking back, that's why I loved him. I always think I cared for all my past boyfriends, but Damian was the one I cared about the most because his love for me was unconditional and never waned.

Damian got out of the car and came and opened my door for me. 'I love you, Damian,' I said, as he helped me out of the car. We held hands right up until the time when I had to be examined by the surgeon. I will never forget his support.

'Will it hurt afterwards?' I nervously asked the surgeon as I sat anxiously on the hospital bed. He was busy tracing lines on my skin where he thought the implants would sit nicely.

'Yes, but we will make sure you have enough painkillers with you when you leave. You just need to make sure you take them as soon as you come to and get lots of rest afterwards,' he explained.

Despite the worry about the pain I might feel afterwards, I was really excited about having new boobs! I knew when I came out of the operating theatre they would give me even more confidence and a better chance to make it as a glamour model. In fact, I couldn't wait to put on the white gown and be wheeled into the theatre. Once I was there, the nurses and the anaesthetist bustled

51

around me. The anaesthetic was then carefully inserted into a tube in my wrist.

At first, I couldn't focus on anything when I came to. 'Are you OK, Cassie?' I heard a muffled voice above me ask. I opened my eyes and a nurse was standing over me, smiling. 'Everything went really well, Cassie. How are you feeling?' she asked.

I could barely make out the outline of her face but I tried to smile. The pain I felt rising up from my chest area was excruciating. I wanted to sit up, but somehow I knew it would only hurt more if I moved.

'Try to relax, darling. The operation went really well. Your boobs will look great. They are swollen and will be quite painful for a week or so,' she explained, handing me two big white pills and a glass of water.

She helped me lift my head and, still staring at the ceiling, I swallowed the pills. I know I have no pain threshold (I can't even squeeze a spot on my face because the pain scares me so much!) but because my operation was carried out under the muscle it hurt like hell.

'Can I see them?' I asked the nurse, trying to look down my body.

'You can try to sit up in half an hour when the painkillers have kicked in,' she explained.

I then started to come to and felt the bandages pressing tightly against my chest. 'I have new boobs!' I smiled to myself and then, as the pain started to subside, nothing else seemed to matter.

Damian came into the room and kissed me. 'You're doing really well, Cassie. You'll be pleased with the result!' He grinned, placing a huge bunch of pink roses on the table next to me. We sat in the hospital room together for the rest of the evening, talking and watching TV.

The next day I was allowed to go home. When I got there I could finally look at my new shape in the mirror. I was still swollen and the bandages didn't allow me to see much, but I felt adrenaline rush through my body when I stood to the side and examined my new silhouette in the mirror. I couldn't wait to take the bandages off, but for the next week I knew all I needed to think about was resting and getting my energy back. I had to take painkillers every four hours and counted down the days until I was to return to Harley Street. Mum didn't say much during that time, but she was kind and caring, and looked after me too.

A week later I went back to see the surgeon. 'They look fantastic, Cassie!' he said, as he slowly unwrapped the bandages.

I felt like an Egyptian mummy woken up from her sleep but sure enough when I saw my new boobs they really were fantastic! 'What do you think, Damian?' I asked, as I paraded my new figure in front of everyone in the room.

'It's really made a huge difference, Cassie. You look fabulous!' he said, smiling.

My waist looked tiny and my shape was totally transformed. I thought of all the new underwear I could buy and how I would at last feel great in a bikini; I just wanted to get out there and show off my new figure. That afternoon I splashed out on underwear, bikinis and skimpy, low-cut dresses. Having surgery was one of the best things I have ever done.

A year or so later, I actually had more surgery and that

was even more painful! I found that I couldn't shift the weight from my stomach and thighs and so I decided to have liposculpture. Liposculpture is a procedure where the surgeons resculpt your body by sucking fat out from under the skin. I found a surgeon who operated in Barcelona and London, and opted for Spain because it was much cheaper over there. Nan came with me on the trip and I was completely black and blue by the end of it all. The surgeon took fat from around my waist and thighs, and also injected more around my bottom so that it lifted up a bit. I spent the next month recovering from that operation because it was quite a big procedure. For days afterwards, I had to wear a wet suit, but it worked and the results looked amazing.

After my initial bout of surgery, I didn't show my new boobs to anyone apart from Damian (and the surgeon, of course!). I wanted to start modelling properly first. I'd also lost weight because, after the recovery period of about six weeks, I started training properly at the local gym and I made sure that I ate well and healthily. I put my heart and soul into making my body as perfect as possible and it felt good when I began to see the results. The next step was getting my modelling career under way and that was the real beginning for me.

Two months after my operation I chose the best shots taken by the Cameo photographer and sent them to top glamour photographer Jeany Savage. Jeany is one of Britain's most established glamour photographers and I found her name in the *Daily Star*. She wrote to me almost straight away and there I was, a week later, standing in front of her in her busy studio in North London! I hadn't asked anyone for advice so I really didn't know what I was letting myself in for, but somehow I knew as soon as I walked into the studio that Jeany Savage was the real McCoy.

'Let me see your body!' she snapped, as I stood waiting in front of her.

Jeany was petite and I could tell immediately that she had once been beautiful. She was still attractive, though, with blonde straight hair and a pretty heart-shaped face. Her small frame didn't mirror her personality, however: Jeany was bold and fiery and dominated the whole room. I stripped down to my thong and stood there in front of her as she quickly eyed me up and down. 'I like it. Get yourself into hair and make-up, choose an outfit from the room over there and we'll start straight away,' she said bluntly, pointing to the back of the room. She then turned round to deal with another model that she was shooting.

Jeany scared the life out of me at the beginning! Being in her studio was completely different from my first test shoot because the Cameo agent had been particularly nice to me and had made sure that I was OK. This time, I could tell it was going to be tougher, but, underneath the nerves, all I wanted to do was pose well and produce some decent shots.

That day there were several models already working with Jeany because she was shooting various projects for the *Daily Star*. I felt so intimidated because there were a few other models standing at the back of the room who'd started glaring at me and whispering. I headed towards them because that was where the make-up girl was working. She was busy making up a busty blonde model in front of a huge mirror, so I sat down on the stool next to them and waited patiently.

'You've just had a boob job, haven't you?' the model piped up.

'Yes, do you like them?' I asked her politely.

'They look OK, but Jeany hates false fingernails. You're in such trouble today – you won't go down well at all,' she replied.

I stared down at my new nails and felt like crying. I thought they looked great, just like my boobs. I couldn't understand what she was talking about – I had done my research and knew that so many of the models I had seen in the papers looked as if they had nail extensions. I reached for a magazine that was lying on the table in front of me and pretended to read. I didn't want to answer the model back or let her see that I was upset, but her cruel words had quickly and unexpectedly stripped away my confidence. At that time she was established in the industry and had started to rake in the money. That day, she was working alongside various other well-known models.

I was, and still am, surprised at how unwelcome the girls made me feel that day. They knew I was a new face and, instead of being bitchy and hostile, they should have been supportive and kind. Amazingly enough, the negative comments that first model had made about my nails were only the start. 'This must be your first time then,' she snapped, eyeing up my face.

'Yes, well, I've already done a test shoot,' I stammered.

'Oh, they never matter! Anyone can do a test shoot – it's what happens after that matters,' she replied and then turned her back on me.

I was so annoyed by that point; the hostility from this girl had, in fact, made me very angry. When it was my turn to be made up, I sat on the stool in silence. I couldn't speak to the make-up girl because I needed to think. I remembered what the Cameo agent had said to me a few months earlier about keeping my head down. I won't let this ruin my chances, I told myself. Just ignore them, keep your head down and be yourself. If the other models feel threatened, so they should be!

When my make-up was finally done, I chose a tiny vest top and briefs, and then walked back into the studio section. I knew my new boobs looked awesome in the top. The other three models were still busy sniggering and whispering to one another, but this time it didn't bother me because I had more important things to think about.

'I need a new girl for Page 3,' Jeany said suddenly, looking straight at me. 'You'll be perfect.'

I glanced over at the other models and saw their jaws drop. There you go, I thought to myself. You were right to feel threatened because I've got what it takes. I'd only come up to do some test shots for Jeany and they had made me feel uncomfortable at first, but there I was already shooting professionally for Page 3! I felt like the cat that got the cream. Later, I found out that the model who had been horrible to me was one of Jeany's favourites, which made my debut model shoot with Jeany Savage even more spectacular.

Throughout my modelling career, I've experienced nastiness and, like I said, it's a very cliquey industry, but I quickly learned how to cope with it and to ignore it. Models are known for stabbing other models in the back:

they can be nice to your face but then compete unashamedly behind your back. They rarely help each other out, they steal one another's boyfriends and they try to ruin each other's chances. For example, at a casting for a TV ad that I later attended, one model told me not to do the casting because it was too sleazy. I believed her and so I walked out of the shoot. The next month when I was watching TV, there she was on that very ad! Eventually, I did make friends with some of the other models, but not that many of them. It didn't bother me, though, because I'd already experienced and dealt with bullying and nastiness at school, so I knew how to ignore it and how to survive with just a few decent friends around me. So, if I didn't gel with any of the girls I came across, or if some of them were bitchy, I knew that, as long as I had a few friends who cared, it didn't matter. Rather than surround myself with loads of friends, I tend to have fewer people in my life at any one time – that way I can devote my energy and time to those few people. Funnily enough, that day at the studio, Jeany never mentioned my nails, so I knew full well that the other girls had just been trying to intimidate me.

Within a week I was on Page 3 – not once, but twice! Everyone saw Jeany's photos and I loved them. Finally, I was somebody and I still remember the excitement I felt when I saw my picture for the first time in the *Daily Star*. My brothers Ben and Conor had been rushing off to the newsagent's every morning, in case my picture should appear that day – and here it was, at last. It was really me, looking great, smiling and confident on Page 3 of a national newspaper!

The next day I called Jeany and thanked her for what she had done for me. 'Don't worry, love,' she said happily. 'I'd love to shoot you more, but I'll really need to book you through a model agent. You could contact a woman called Yvonne Paul and she'll take a look at you.'

'Thanks,' I replied and, after I'd written down Yvonne's number, I called her to arrange a meeting.

A week later, I went to see Yvonne. I knew she was a respected and famous model agent so I made sure I was fully prepared. I got my hair cut and styled, and had a French manicure. Arriving at her office, I felt confident when I pressed the buzzer.

'Come on up,' said a woman's voice.

I climbed the stars and knocked at the door. When I entered the room, Yvonne was flicking through a model book. She didn't even look up. 'Sit down. You must be Cassie,' she said. So I sat down on the sofa in front of her and waited. I looked at her and then looked slowly around the room. Yvonne was small and wore glasses, and again, just like Jeany Savage, I thought she looked like she had once been a model. Behind her, the wall was plastered with photos of glamour girls. I could see names like Katie Price and Nell McAndrew beneath the faces that stared back at me, smiling. It was all so inspiring for me as I thought about the glittering career that possibly lay ahead.

'Jeany has recommended you, which is a great start,' Yvonne suddenly said, still looking at the black book in front of her. 'Let me see what pictures you've got.'

I pulled my photos out of my bag and handed them to her. 'The first thing you need to do is get yourself a decent book. Then we'll get some more shots done of you and a contacts card, and I'll start getting you some work. Will you do implied nude and topless?' she asked.

'I'm not sure what that is,' I said.

'It's where you pose nude, but you can't see anything,' she said, eyeing me up and down.

'I won't do fully nude, that's all,' I replied.

'OK, well I'll be in touch soon,' she said.

With that, I knew it was time for me to leave. I felt pleased that Yvonne seemed to want to get me work, but when I left her office that day I felt like I was swimming in a sea of nothingness.

At the time, I was still only 18 and nothing had been explained to me about the modelling industry or what the job entailed. I didn't know what to expect, how much I could earn or how to get on and make a success of myself. Looking back, I wish I'd been more assertive about hassling my agent for work but I was still unsure of myself. Had I been less reticent, I think I could have generated more work for myself. Of course, I was happy that Yvonne had taken me on and that I had got myself an agent but, as time went on, it became clearer to me that, to make ends meet and to make a mark in the industry, I'd need to do it all myself and would have to find a way on my own to survive the hardships that cropped up.

Looking back, it still shocks me that even those people who control the glamour industry and were perhaps models themselves don't have a structured plan to guide and protect the girls they sign up and from whom they make their living. They make their money but they don't do enough to nurture and protect these innocent new models in the process. To this day, it pains me to think that no one is there to offer hands-on advice on potentially difficult aspects of the modelling trade, such as starting a new life in London and getting settled into a new freelance job when money is often tight for the first few years. Like many other young models, I was young and from a small town; I'd never experienced modelling or London before – or the type of cut-throat characters who drive the industry forward. I never realised I wouldn't earn enough money at the start or that I'd come face to face with a very superficial and decadent crowd. I wish I'd been warned about the dangers of drugs and partying; that I'd been taught how to handle the press and had known how the media might label a model – for example, if they ventured into the world of hostessing to make ends meet. Now I fully understand why a lot of young models fall by the wayside or fail because there's no one around to advise them at the start. Most young models are much too vulnerable to deal with the job alone and many buckle under the pressure and never reach their potential because of their inability to understand and work the industry to their advantage. I really believe things need to change and someone must take responsibility.

Regardless of my fear of the unknown and without any real guidance, I was still determined to follow my dream. I found it within me to push myself forward as much as I could, and as best I could on my own. All I knew was that I had to make regular calls to Yvonne most mornings about work. 'Have you got anything for me today, Yvonne?' I'd ask her anxiously.

Normally she would let me know what shoot I was booked on and where it was in London. She would also tell me what I needed to wear, the time and fee; the rest was up to me. If the shoot was that afternoon, I would always be ready. Every night I would check that my nails looked perfect and my hair was clean and glossy. By that point, I had started having regular facials and, because I was training regularly at the gym, I was in great shape too. Whenever I hopped on the train to London, I also always made sure that I knew exactly where I was going before I left!

Each kind of shoot was different – the Page 3 shoots are really organised and there would often be five models there at the same time, each with our own time slot. It was straight into hair and make-up, into your pants and heels and then out in front of the camera for a maximum of twenty minutes. Magazine shoots, on the other hand, could take a whole day. Plus, you might be the only model on the shoot and have to do several underwear changes and lots of different poses.

As soon as I started to build up my portfolio, Damian was a sweetheart and bought me my own book. I remember staring down at the new black portfolio and feeling so happy. 'That means such a lot to me!' I smiled, kissing him. That day we sorted through all my photos and slotted the best ones we could find into the clean plastic sleeves. There were hundreds of glamour shots of me from Page 3 and various feature shoots I'd done for *FHM*, *Loaded* and *Front* magazines. When we finally closed the book and it was packed full of pictures, I realised that I was actually doing really well! 'I'm so happy, Damian,' I told him that night.

'I am too, Cassie,' he said, kissing my cheek. 'You're doing so well already.'

And he was right: the modelling had started to work and I was earning at least £500 a week. The quality of my photos was good and they were getting me more work. I'd also started to build up more work through doing test shoots where photographers trying to break into the industry needed to shoot models for free. I knew my name was quickly circulating around the UK media as a top glamour model and that editors and casting agents were interested in shooting me.

The first six months were hectic. I shot for all the best magazines and was told that there was interest in me abroad. *Playboy* was constantly talking to Yvonne about me and I was always being offered various major lingerie campaigns. I was still living at home and so I didn't need a lot of money, and I was saving for the first time. I wanted to repay Damian for all the support he had given me so I spent money on nights out with him and bought him presents whenever I could. I'd also bought myself a little car so we could spend weekends away together. At that point I was so content with my life that it was surprising when, a few months later, things couldn't have become more different.

Chapter Five

Professional Party Girl

WHEN I JOINED YVONNE PAUL, IT FELT EXCITING BECAUSE I'D OFFICIALLY STARTED MY MODELLING CAREER. Although I didn't know what to expect and felt out of my depth, that feeling of the unknown was still thrilling for me. The reason I dived in headfirst was because I knew there was a whole new glamorous world waiting for me up in London. I'd been captivated by what I'd already seen and heard; also I'd noticed the sheer volume of money that drove the modelling business forward and had been told about the celebrity world that attached itself to it. And I loved the glamour that shrouded everything so completely. It felt as if this luxurious lifestyle was right at my fingertips and I was lured in fast.

At this time I was still in awe of the other models that I met. Whenever I was at a photo shoot I'd notice how fashionable and glamorous they were. They were always perfectly groomed and totally gorgeous! They'd sit and chat with the make-up girls about the parties they'd gone to the night before, their mega-rich boyfriends and the amazing celebrities they were meeting on a daily basis. 'We went to Chinawhite last night! Puff Daddy was in there, surrounded by girls. He spotted me and told me he loved my dress!' I remember one model saying gleefully. She sat and chattered animatedly about the champagne that had flowed all night and the flamboyant after-party that followed. I wondered if I'd ever be a part of the dazzling world that she was describing. I knew that because I too was a model, it wasn't out of my reach, but at that point I didn't know how to get there.

During my first few months as a model, a burning desire to taste the exciting world that I was hearing about overcame me. At the time I probably thought it would fill the void within me that had perhaps been created by Papa. This world had such a huge pull and attraction that I assumed it would give me the security I so desperately craved as a child. It seemed that the models I knew were made to feel special and beautiful, and for them, everything was just perfect. I actually began to think about it so much that I then started to feel depressed about my life back home in Sheppey. It consisted of going to the same clubs and pubs and seeing the same people every weekend. Day in, day out, I would have the same conversations with the same old crowd and it was starting to bore me. There was none of the glamour, money, celebrities or luxury that the other models had talked about. In comparison, my life seemed so dull. I quickly realised that Sheppey wasn't 'me' any more and that I didn't want the small house with the babies or to shop on a Saturday afternoon with Damian on Sheerness High Street. I wanted to live the life that the other fun-loving, glamorous models were living. Unlike me, they weren't a Sheppey statistic – they were out networking with celebrities every night; they had confidence, independence and seemed as if they were going places. They were out there trying to fulfil their dreams and being swooned over by amazing men. I realised that I needed to be upfront with Damian about how I felt and to ask him if he wanted to join my journey with me.

One night I finally opened up to him about my worries. 'I need different things in my life, Damian,' I told him, as we lay in bed together. 'Sheppey is holding me back and I'm not happy here any more. I want more excitement in my life and the modelling I've been doing up in London has shown me that. It's changed me, Damian, and I'd like us to start a new life together, perhaps up there.'

But Damian looked over at me and just smiled, saying, 'I understand, Cassie. I'm happy with the way we are, though. Let's decide what we should do once your work picks up a bit more.' He then kissed me goodnight.

I remember feeling pleased that he was being nice about what I'd said, but, because I knew Damian wouldn't ever want to change our lifestyle despite now having an opportunity to, I'd already made my own decision. That night I decided that I would move off the island and away from him. I needed – and wanted – to experience the bright lights of London, alone. For me, Sheppey had suddenly become a closed chapter and, sadly, Damian was also part of that. I wanted more from life.

By this time I had by chance started a friendship with a man called Luke, a scaffolder who I'd met at a local pub. Luke was in his late twenties and looked a bit rough and ready. He was a friend, but I'd seen qualities in him that I wanted to see in Damian. Luke was ambitious and he had drive; he was independent and people looked up to him. He had his own house and made a decent living; he provided for himself and that was starting to matter to me. A few years down the line and Damian would have been happy to have a small house, two kids, a holiday once a year and to see the same people all the time, but that wasn't good enough for me any more.

One day things got out of hand because I'd visited Luke's house without telling Damian. That day I'd needed to pour my heart out to someone and because Luke was older, I'd gone to him. I hadn't thought much about the implications of spending time with another man and I know that was bad of me.

'There is someone at the door for you, Cassie,' Luke told me, as I sat drinking a cup of tea in his living room.

I went to the front door and saw Damian standing there, looking upset.

'What are you doing here, Cassie?' he asked quietly. 'Are you being unfaithful to me?'

'Oh, Damian,' I replied, concerned. 'It's not what you think at all. I needed someone to talk to. Let's go home.'

I got my bag and then told Luke I had to go. He knew what had happened so he just smiled and told me to call him if I needed to. I remember my mind was clouded when I drove back to Mum's. Damian was behind me in his car and I could see his sad, scared face in the mirror. I knew that this was make or break. On arriving home, we went up to the bedroom to talk. He told me his friend had seen my car outside Luke's house and had called him up, so he'd rushed round to get me. 'I'm hurt that you got close to another man, Cassie. I know you didn't cheat on me so I'm not angry, but please promise me that you won't see Luke again,' Damian said.

I froze because, although he was being understanding and kind, I felt that he didn't really understand what I was going through. This wasn't about Luke at all: it was about my having changed and wanting different things in my life and Damian not wanting to join me on the journey.

That night I told Damian that we needed to part. 'I need to be alone and to focus on my modelling. I don't think you really want to be a part of the change. I need that excitement I told you about and I need this change,' I stammered, trying to get every reason out clearly.

Damian went silent. 'I understand, Cassie, and, because I love you, I need to let you go – I can't leave my life here,' I remember him saying calmly.

That night, we both cried in each other's arms in bed. Damian and I had been through so much together and we did have a love that was deep, but it was the end of an era for us. I'd wanted him to experience this journey with me but, when I knew he didn't want to change his life with me, I realised that he would only hold me back.

The next morning he packed his things and left. To this day I will always be thankful for Damian: he didn't make a scene and he allowed me to follow my dreams. As difficult as it was for him, he supported my needs and I will never forget the courage that it took for him to do that. I still felt a huge loss when I left Damian because he added something to my life. I'd lost Papa and, now, because of my dreams, I'd lost Damian too, but I quickly managed to fill the void.

Strangely enough, that same day a lovely new person came into my life. I was busy changing out of my underwear at the end of an *FHM* shoot when a model approached me and started to chat. She was pretty, bubbly and oozed confidence. I liked her immediately. 'Are you new?' she asked, smiling. 'I'm Stacey. I noticed you when you came into the studio today and thought you looked great. It's hard at the start, love, but it gets easier when you get your face about and you start to make friends.'

I had lost Damian that day and, boy, did I need a friend! I hadn't met anyone so far and I welcomed Stacey into my life straight away.

So Stacey Gunshon became my first proper friend in the glamour industry. She worked at Stringfellows nightclub in central London, which at that time was a glamorous hangout. I remember feeling intrigued by her and her job. 'What's it like, stripping?' I asked her as we caught the tube together one day.

'It's great fun, but people do look down on the job. I strip because I can't make ends meet modelling. I like to model and to go out on the scene but I also need money for that and I make a ton more money at Stringfellows. It makes my quality of life perfect. I don't lie about it and I get on with it – it's all interlinked in the end and a lot of girls do it,' she explained happily.

Until that day I had never thought about stripping, but when Stacey told me she could earn up to £2,000 a night

I began to grill her about the job. I had never seen that amount of money in my bank account and the thought that I could make that kind of money in a day intrigued me. It all sounded so fantastic, especially when she told me that one punter often spent £2,000 just so he could chat to her!

'You need to audition, though. Usually the girls turn up and have to dance in front of Peter, the owner. You need buckets of confidence and to know how to handle men. Sometimes you get a lot of hassle from the punters,' she warned. I knew then that it wasn't for me. For one thing, I couldn't dance, plus I would never have the guts to stand up in front of men and dance. At that point, I was also far from expert when it came to handling men, too!

I admired – and still admire – Stacey's confidence and courage, but it was because she was honest and secure with herself that she stayed sane. Stacey loved modelling, partying and money, and she found a way to sustain all three. She kept a balance in her life and had no expectations from the glamour world, and that's why she never suffered. Because she knew this world had its limitations and can sometimes be filled with empty promises, she never fell into the trap of being too idealistic. She earned a good living but she kept her head down and was strong enough to fight off the demons alone. One night I went to watch her working and she was awesome, but that was only because she was so proud of who she was and what she did.

Later on in my career, I discovered that many models stripped simply to keep themselves on track, just as Stacey had done. In fact, many of them did whatever they had to just to follow their dreams but then suffered the consequences. Most young glamour models begin their journey by believing, as I did, that their dreams are within their grasp but only a few really make it because the rest get swayed elsewhere. They are sold empty promises when they start out; they hear stories of glamour, money and luxury, but, as they travel further into the world they so desperately crave, they realise that only a rare few of them become a real part of that world. Along the way, many quickly fall off the rails because they just can't keep up. If they do taste the glamour and the glitz, then it's normally because they are busy ruining their lives dabbling in other things and it's only a taste that they get. Many models try to make ends meet by doing escorting or stripping and they also start to go out and about on the party circuit as a way of getting their names about.

Unless a model is made aware of the financial and personal limitations, and is shown how to survive the pitfalls and avoid the sharks out there, then embarking on this journey can be like a train crash waiting to happen. And that's exactly what happened to me. Like many before me, I also fell into the abyss and my dream of making it as a glamour model almost became forgotten.

At this point, I was still missing Damian. I remember that it was tough not having any close friends at work, so one day I felt that I needed to talk about my feelings to Stacey. 'I left my boyfriend last week,' I confided in her. I had been feeling very low because I still loved Damian.

'We're going out tonight then. Come to mine tonight, we'll get ready together and we'll make a whole night of it. You need this, Cassie. It'll take your mind off things for a while,' Stacey said. She had known exactly what to do and it meant more than anything to me that day that she cared about me.

The other thing that was amazing about Stacey was how she cared about my modelling work and, because I didn't understand the industry, she was worried about how I'd cope with the distractions she knew would crop up around me. She knew how important, personally and professionally, going out that night was, but she also understood that I needed to be careful. 'It's so important to be seen out, Cassie. It'll help build your profile, but you need to watch the partying because it's addictive and can sidetrack you. It has been known to ruin girls,' she warned. Stacey had explained to me before then how working as a model meant that it was crucial that I got out and met the right people, that it was important that my name became known on the scene because that would help me get established, but she stressed again and again that I needed to balance out the late nights with hard work. I had no idea what she had meant at the start, but at that point I just accepted what she said and carried on. She was always so perceptive, helpful and thoughtful, and that meant so much to me. To this day, although I didn't follow her advice about finding a balance, I will always owe Stacey a great deal just because she cared.

I'd longed to see the inside of a London nightclub. In fact, during our photo shoot that day it was all I could think about and it lifted my spirits considerably. I'd heard so many exciting stories about the party scene as I'd listened in on other models' conversations, and had read about so many wild and wonderful things in the tabloids. The names of places such as Chinawhite would ring in my ears and I'd often wonder if those clubs and the people who went to them were like I always imagined: wall-to-wall beautiful people, flowing champagne and amazing clothes and jewellery.

After the shoot I caught the train home and trawled through my wardrobe, looking for something special to wear. At the time I didn't have many clothes but I was in great shape and so I knew I could wear just about anything on my first night out and still look sexy. I quickly packed a few things into an overnight bag and caught an early-evening train back up to London.

When I arrived at Stacey's I couldn't wait to start getting ready.

'Cassie, wear whatever you want! Pick whatever you feel like,' Stacey smiled, as she hugged me tightly.

I stared into her bulging wardrobe. It was packed full of Roberto Cavalli dresses and Jimmy Choo shoes! Stacey was in the kitchen, opening a bottle of champagne, and, after eyeing up her dresses, I picked an amazing red Dior dress and a pair of matching stiletto heels. Already I felt like a million dollars, just imagining myself in the dress, before slipping it quickly over my head. As we sipped our champagne, we set to work doing our hair and make-up. 'You're a model and you're going to party hard tonight,' I whispered to myself, as I took one last glance in the mirror: the red dress fitted me perfectly and the end result looked stunning.

We caught a black cab to a club called The Wellington in Knightsbridge. I hadn't heard of it before, but Stacey told me it was the 'in' place to go. Funnily enough, The Wellington was later to become my home, but that night I was nervous as I walked down the small flight of steps for the very first time and the doormen quickly waved us in.

On entering the club, I was star-struck straight away. My hands were shaking with nerves as I spotted celebrities such as Max Beesley and Freddie Ljungberg drinking and chatting at the bar. The top fashion model Sophie Anderton and her boyfriend at that time, Mark Bosnich, were sipping Cristal champagne in the corner. They looked so gorgeous together. There were also various *EastEnders* stars, like Dean Gaffney, and pop stars such as Simon Webbe and Duncan James from the boy band Blue. In fact, there were good-looking, fit men everywhere, dressed smartly in Gucci suits and crisp, fitted white shirts. Around me, the women I could see all looked stunning and were draped in Versace and Dior. Later, I discovered that the men were mostly footballers, the women actresses and models. I didn't know their names or recognise all of their faces but that night Stacey told me that the people around me were the main part of the London party scene. I remember feeling I was in heaven as I watched good-looking men come up and chat to Stacey. 'This is Cassie,' she would say when they asked who I was, introducing me to anyone and everyone. 'She's the new face on the block and is a great girl.' As we stood waiting for our drinks at the bar, I remember feeling in awe of her because I could tell everyone knew her and loved her company. Stacey was so cool to be around too. I was careful not to seem star-struck around her but I was... completely! That night Stacey literally ran around the club introducing me to everyone that she possibly could and after an hour I was happily sipping champagne and relaxing with my new friends.

That night Stacey and I partied at The Wellington well into the early hours. By the time the club shut at 3am, I felt confident and at ease – and all I wanted to do was carry on partying! My prayers were answered when Stacey told me we were going on somewhere else. 'There's an after-party at someone's house,' she smiled. 'He's a bigwig in the music industry!' It turned out that the then model Calum Best had invited us to go with him and so we ended up sharing a cab up to a posh house in North London.

When we arrived at the house it was very grand. I walked in, holding Stacey's hand, and spotted a grand piano sitting in the state-of-the-art, immaculate hallway. The walls were covered with thousands of gold and platinum record discs, the rooms heaving with people, who smiled and greeted us warmly. Stacey and I helped ourselves to champagne and then sat down on a huge sofa in the living room to chat.

'Are they taking cocaine over there?' I remember asking her.

'Probably. It's normal, Cassie,' she explained. 'It's all part of the scene.'

I wasn't surprised at her answer and drugs were nothing new to me anyway. I'd already tried cocaine once when I'd been out with Damian at the local pub in Sheppey but I'd taken drugs mainly because I was bored. Back then, I could take them or leave them.

At the local in Sheppey, cocaine had got me high and that had been fun, but that night in North London I experienced something completely different. I remember that, soon after asking Stacey about the cocaine, I was suddenly approached by a friendly man, who gave me my first line of cocaine in London. 'Here, Cassie, this one is for you,' he said, smiling, as he chopped up a thin line of cocaine on the glass table in front of us. He was polite and kind, and seemed to want us to have a good time, nothing more, nothing less. I accepted the rolled-up £50 note he handed me and inhaled the cocaine from the tabletop. I remember my mind cleared straight away and, as my front teeth tingled, I felt euphoric as I stared, wide-eyed, around the crowded room. 'If you want any more, just come and find me,' said the man, as he wandered off into the kitchen.

I realised that night that to those people offering someone a line of cocaine was like offering someone a drink or a cigarette. Despite the cocaine on offer, I didn't take any more that night, though, because I didn't need to. The combination of glamour, cocaine, champagne and friendly, beautiful people had taken me to a level I never ever thought possible. I felt so special and at that time I really felt like it filled a void within me. In fact, I'd never ever felt so fantastic and happy.

I fell in love with my new party life and was soon hooked. It made me feel secure, beautiful and wanted, just like a boyfriend would make his girlfriend feel, just like a father would make his daughter feel. Partying stopped me feeling isolated and alone. Within a month, I met everyone, all of whom took cocaine and simply lived to party. They seemed so confident and alive and I wanted to fit in and become like them. There were top DJs, well-known models, TV stars, music producers and pop stars. Whenever there was a party, I'd stay over at Stacey's and we soon got ourselves into a nice little routine of working during the days and going out together at night. 'What are we doing tonight, Stacey?' I'd say, whenever we woke up together. Sometimes, even though we might have been out the night before and I was hungover and tired, I wanted more because I was having such fun. We would go to barbecues and drinks parties at apartments costing millions at the weekends or on the days when we weren't working, and then we would head out to clubs and after-parties at night. Normally we would go out on a Wednesday night, a Friday and a Saturday. There was always something fabulous going on in London and Stacey would always be invited.

It was a few months after my first night out with Stacey that she took me to my first penthouse party. 'There's a bash at a penthouse in Northwest London tonight, Cassie. It should be good because everyone who's anyone is going,' I remember her saying sleepily one morning after we'd woken up.

And, so, that night our usual routine began. At 8pm we turned on her sound system and happily sipped our champagne. Then Stacey and I began to get ready together as we buzzed with excitement. I remember being overwhelmed when we arrived at that particular party. 'This place is truly amazing,' I gasped, as we entered the penthouse flat in Camden. I looked over to the glass doors and noticed they opened out on to a stunning 200ft roof terrace. The art-deco-designed room was packed with beautiful people, all drinking cocktails. Stacey and I immediately started to mingle and, before I knew it, it was dawn. There was a lot of cocaine there and that was the first time that I actually stayed at a party for 24 hours. By the end of the day the beautiful and confident people I'd seen when I first entered 24 hours beforehand had now become my best friends. After a while it became normal for me to meet and make friends with random people at parties like the one in Camden. But that was the London scene: it made you feel special and loved by everyone around you. Everyone was in it together and that made me feel as if I finally belonged somewhere. The bullies at school and Papa were a million miles away, but looking back, I was slowly losing my way.

One night I went to another interesting after-party. I'd been at Chinawhite with Stacey, where we'd met a cute City boy. 'Come back and party with me!' he'd said, smiling, and I remember suddenly finding myself in a huge floodlit pool at his mansion.

'Come on, Cassie!' I remember the brunette shouting. 'It's really warm in here.'

I stripped off and was wearing a pink lace thong and bra. I then jumped into the floodlit swimming pool. The other two girls were busy splashing one another in the deep end and I couldn't wait to join in the fun. I swam over to the girls and watched as they messed about in the water. The City boy was standing at the other end of the pool, shouting and egging them on.

Suddenly I felt the brunette's hand snake around my waist and I was soon struggling for breath as she pulled me underwater. I broke free and swam to the surface. I swam to the side of the pool and laughed. 'Throw me a towel!' I called out to the City boy, as the two girls continued to frolic in the pool.

After that night of fun, I would often return to the City boy's place for luxurious poolside after-parties. His house was so huge that it was conducive to holding the most opulent of parties and we made the most of it whenever we could. I remember that there were marble floors and huge bathrooms. Normally, when the clubs shut, twenty of us would head back there and get into the pool in our underwear just as I had done on that first night. There were lights at the bottom of the pool and you could look up at the sky through the glass ceiling. The City boy would stand at the bar mixing his cocktails while his friends would offer drugs, including cocaine and weed. People would take the cocaine, try to relax using the weed and then crash out in the bedrooms.

It was during the first year of my modelling career, when I was still only 19 years old, that I also began partying in hotel rooms – but that was a different ballgame altogether. Sometimes whoever was hosting an after-party at a hotel would often book a couple of rooms in one of the top London hotels. Random people would invite me out when I was out at a club. I remember my first inauguration into the world of hotel parties and how I discovered that most of them would turn into full-blown sex orgies. The first one I attended, I was brave enough to go it alone. 'Thanks for the lift, Stacey,' I'd said to her as I climbed out of the cab that night. 'Are you sure you don't want to come in with me? It'll be fun. Please come up with me,' I begged her.

'No, I've got a big day tomorrow and then Strings tomorrow night. You go on in and enjoy yourself, sweetheart. I'll ring you tomorrow before I leave for work.'

I knew she wasn't going to budge because she had already pushed up the cab window and was soon heading off down Park Lane. I remember feeling alone on the pavement and for a moment I felt nervous, but when I thought of the celebrities who might be at the party the excitement changed my mood.

I remember that when I strolled through the revolving glass door and into the exquisite hotel lobby my heart was beating heavily. The man at the club had told me where to go, but suddenly I was alone and unsure of what to expect that night. You could have heard a pin drop as I nervously pressed the lift button and was carried to the top floor. The room was full of models and footballers.

'Hey, Cassie!' shouted one of the footballers as I walked further into the huge suite. 'Love the dress. Are you on your own tonight?' he asked and grinned as he undressed me with his eyes.

I'd met him a few weeks earlier at The Wellington. He was a foreign player and quite young so it was obvious that he'd got swept up in the scene quite quickly because he always seemed to be out. All I knew about him was that he had a reputation in the club for using escorts. At that point I didn't know how or when, but as I looked around the hotel suite that night I assumed there would be a few girls working because his crowd were known for being like that.

'How are you?' I asked.

'Everything's good. Are you here all night?' he asked, moving closer. He was dark and good-looking and if I hadn't heard the rumours about him I would have probably stayed a bit longer and chatted.

'No, I'm just here for a nightcap,' I replied. With that, I turned and walked further into the room.

I remember the suite was huge and luxurious. There were four bedrooms off the main room. I noticed there was a pyramid of cocaine on the main table and drinks laid out on the side. Everything was obviously free but it was usual for the host to supply drink and drugs for all his guests. I looked around the room for a familiar face but I didn't recognise anyone apart from the footballer. Perhaps someone I know will be in one of the bedrooms, I said to myself, and wandered over to the first door. It was slightly ajar and what I saw that night will always stay fixed in my memory. Through the door, a girl lay sprawled naked on the king-sized bed. She wasn't smiling, but she was concentrating on the semi-clothed man lying beneath her. At the side of the bed another man handed him a deodorant bottle. The man inserted it in her and she smiled. I then noticed three other men walking towards the en-suite bathroom. They stepped over an empty Coca-Cola bottle that had been discarded on the floor. I remember feeling vomit surge into my throat so I turned away and headed straight back to the safety of the living room.

When I spotted a friend of mine from The Wellington, I soon forgot about the girl and the voyeurs who were still with her in the bedroom. Later on, however, I noticed that every once in a while a different man would walk into the bedroom where the girl was. I did feel sorry for her that night, but then it seemed to me that she would have left the party if she hadn't wanted to do it.

After that night, walking in on sex orgies like that one became normal for me and, although I never got involved, they rarely shocked me as much as the first time at the hotel. I grew to understand that, because the people who I partied with took so many drugs, they were so much more into group sex and because I was a part of that scene it felt normal. After that I'd notice girls pairing off with men, often three at a time. These girls would turn up at parties already high on cocaine. They would then take random men into bedrooms because they didn't know what they were doing. Threesomes and sexual voyeurism were normal even if they'd just met because cocaine blew all boundaries and that night was no exception. Then there were the escorts that came into the picture as I delved deeper into the scene. I'd noticed them that first hotel party night when I was happily mingling with the other guests there. 'Can I get three of your best girls?' one of the City boys had said loudly on his mobile. He was buzzing from cocaine and had already told everyone in the room that he needed to have sex with a woman that night. He knew that none of the girls already at the party was up for it, so he had obviously called up an agency. Within half an hour, three young girls were standing in a row in the hotel-room doorway. 'I'll take you two,' he'd said, pointing to a Chinese girl and a curvy blonde. The other brunette stared blankly back at him and then wandered off into the night. The City boy took the two girls into another bedroom and, again, other men joined them later as the night progressed.

It was morning when I finally left that hotel suite. I remember the sun had burst through the penthouse window and I shielded my sore eyes. It was almost 10am and everyone was either asleep or still up drinking and sniffing cocaine. I realised I needed to go and so I wandered towards the bathroom, where I washed my face and then headed towards the door. It was my first all-night sex party and, despite feeling hungover when the sun came up, I'd really enjoyed being there.

The other models I'd made friends with that night laughed as I said goodbye. 'You're now going to do the "Walk of Shame", Cassie!' they exclaimed.

I nodded in agreement, but had no idea what they meant until I walked through the hotel lobby feeling shattered. I was wearing the same clothes as the night before and, as I saw the receptionist watch my every step, I thought he must have smelled the alcohol on my breath and the drugs on my clothes. It felt like everyone in the lobby was staring at me. They probably were, but then that's why the model world calls it the Walk of Shame. And that was my very first one!

I remember that I did miss Damian that morning when I finally arrived home, but, when I started to look forward to the next party and perhaps seeing my new friends again, my mood quickly lifted and the feeling of emptiness that I had first felt about him disappeared.

Chapter Six

Natalie

As my passion for modelling grew stronger, so too did my passion for partying and the glamorous scene. I soon wanted to become a real part of the lavish London party crowd and not just someone who dipped in and out of it, as I did. The whole party scene captivated me and it gave me a place. I loved the stylish, beautiful people, the money and fast cars. And I also loved the designer clothes and free-thinking mentality. It was highly addictive and got a hold of me very quickly. I'd dreamed about tasting this scene so much, and now there I was, finally on the edge of it and ready to dive in properly.

At this point, I'd still only been modelling for less than a year. I was working hard and getting regular model bookings for *Playboy*, Page 3 and all the lads' magazines. But, despite my heavy workload, I still wasn't making any more money than I had at the start and that had begun to frustrate me. The opulent lifestyle, where success and money were staring me in the face felt so near, but they were still so far from my grasp. I was living the party lifestyle and had successful and moneyed friends, but I definitely couldn't finance it as they could. At this time I really focused on becoming fully immersed in it, so I could perhaps become like them.

I still remembered what Stacey had told me at the start of my career. 'Being a model is tough at the start and it takes years to cut it. You might get tempted by the glamour of the party scene and that might help you get more work, but this side of the industry will eventually get you down. If you get sucked in and party too much, it will eat away at your finances and then at your sanity,' she repeated, over and over again. 'I told you, Cassie,' she would say whenever I felt depressed about not having enough money. 'You just can't make ends meet on a glamour model's wage. You can't party like this either. You might need to subsidise your wages with another job until you start getting bigger modelling contracts.'

Stacey was right, but, as I said, I certainly didn't want to get another job after all I'd gone through. With that in mind I decided my first option was to network harder. Becoming known on the scene did produce results. I knew models who were better off than me simply because they partied. They got their names and faces into the press and in turn this brought them more work; they knew editors and photographers and it was those contacts that I needed to work on. I knew it was getting expensive, but I was already mixing with the right crowd and so I assumed that, if I attended every party going in London and made sure that people knew me, I too would become a 'face'. I knew from other models that, if you were a popular model on the scene and a regular party girl, the media took notice of you. It was the media who booked me for most of my work and who drove this industry forward, so I needed them to see me. Six months into my modelling career and I felt confident about my next plan of action. I decided to throw my all into the London party scene, hoping that things would then start to improve professionally and therefore financially for me, but I know looking back that I was just kidding myself and was already making poor decisions alone.

It was when I met Natalie Denning that things changed even more as far as the work–party balance was concerned. Although we both spent time working hard, the partying really took over. 'I've seen your face at Chinas,' I remember a petite blonde model saying as she smiled at me. 'We should go out together some time, if you like?' There was Natalie, standing confidently in front of me in Yvonne's office, and I remember her being very pretty and having these amazing catlike, sparkly blue eyes.

'Sure,' I replied. 'What's your name?'

I was initially wary of her because of the look in her eyes. Her eyes looked dangerous and gave little away, so at that point I couldn't decide whether she was trustworthy or not. Surprisingly, then, she and I went on to become like sisters as we held hands through an exciting but difficult transition in our lives. I relied on Natalie and she relied on me as we set about mastering the modelling industry together. When our friendship sadly came to an end later on, it cut me like a knife.

The great thing that Natalie and I gave each other was different strengths. I taught her to wear her heart on her sleeve and to let go a bit more; she taught me how to hang on in there and to keep trying when modelling jobs failed to materialise. Also, while I tended to let life take its course, Natalie was much more proactive. She was very ambitious, almost ruthless at times. I found that tough to deal with sometimes, but I always admired her for her tenacity and determination. Natalie and I were in fact the perfect match: young, ambitious models who wanted to party. Both small-town girls, we were equally impressed by the bright lights of London. We had also both just split from our first loves and wanted to move away from home for the first time.

We had met a couple of times after the first shoot we did together, which was a storyboard feature for the *News of the World*. We'd swapped numbers and had chatted on the phone a few times since then, and then we met again on a film shoot. During those times, we had discussed the modelling industry a lot together and we had already started to learn how tough and fickle it was. Both of us had encountered bitching from other models and felt that we weren't being guided sufficiently.

Out of the blue one day Natalie asked me to move in. She'd said it suddenly as she looked at me from where she sat in the make-up chair. We were doing a photo shoot together and were already fond of one another, despite only having known each other a few weeks. I looked at her and didn't even need to think. 'Sure, when?' I asked and that was it, Natalie and I were suddenly starting our new lives together. At the time, I wasn't worried about the fact that we hadn't known one another very long. We got on well, wanted the same lifestyle in London and shared the same dreams.

Over time, to me it was a given that we would stick our necks out for one another. I trusted Natalie for dear life and, as I put all my energy into the friendship with her, at the start it worked. I would invite her to do modelling jobs with me and she did the same. The first job I landed for us was perfect because it gave us time to really bond together.

'Come with me, Nat, please,' I remember begging her down the phone.

'What is it?' she asked excitedly.

'It's a glamorous event called the Gumball Rally. The magazine needs two gorgeous models to party with their clients along the route. It will be sheer luxury. They have said they will book us into five-star hotels and we will get photographed anywhere we like if we go. It might be the perfect opportunity for us to meet new high-profile people and get noticed,' I explained.

Nat didn't need much persuading and it was at this event that we really got to know one another, as we enjoyed the party of all parties. We were already flat-hunting and this was taking up a lot of our time so the event would provide a nice break for us both. We packed our bags and set off with the Gumball drivers from London. The route would last a week, stopping at places like Paris and Monaco. For a whole week we partied together, travelling with celebrities, racing drivers and the richest of people, who worked for companies like Ferrari, Lamborghini and Bentley. The event was highly luxurious and we fitted in perfectly.

Just as I helped Natalie with modelling work and attending events like Gumball, she also helped me. She was more streetwise than I was and also persistent about us moving forward. Already she had had a taste of the celebrity world: she had had a fling with an A-list Hollywood star in Paris about a year before I met her, and had a few photographer friends already. She knew the ropes more than I did and was kind enough to share her connections with me. For example, Natalie told me she knew a good glamour photographer called George Richardson. 'All we need to do is show up at his studio and pose for him. He will market and sell our shots, and then pay us,' she explained, a week after we got back from Monaco.

It was great because, after we met George that week, he sold shots of us to all the UK press and we started to make a name as a twosome.

Following that shoot we focused hard on getting a flat together. We didn't want to be apart, plus it was becoming more pressing for us to be in London for work and the parties. We wanted to continue to do the photo shoots with George and also have fun together while we networked. All we needed was a bed and somewhere to sleep because we knew that, if we were up in London, we would be out partying and working a lot.

When Natalie found the Liverpool Street bed-sit, she persuaded me to take it with her. 'It's only temporary,' Natalie had said, smiling, her hand on my arm. 'Listen, we will be here together and we just need to sleep here, that's all. It's just until we really find our feet and start to make proper money.'

90

Natalie

I looked around the room and sighed. It was a horrible little room and I hated it, but Natalie was right. I knew we wouldn't be there forever because everything was changing so fast and we were definitely on a new and exciting path together. I knew that, if we took on the Liverpool Street bed-sit, it would only be a stopgap. After all, there are more important things to spend our money on than a nicer place, I told myself, and so we put down our deposit straight away. Back in those days, I was incredibly spontaneous and didn't give the future a great deal of thought – my main objective was to have fun!

There were five other bedrooms in the house, which were rented out by foreign guys. I look back and think we were lucky in there, as we never had any trouble from them. The room must have been 9ft x 9ft. There was an old dirty mattress on the floor and no bedding. We moved in at the end of 2002 and put our two suitcases next to the mattress and made that room our home. We decided we would eat out when we could and just come back there to sleep. More like a squat than a home, it was dire and depressing, but Natalie and I had each other so nothing mattered. We grew close very quickly because we were on top of one another. You need someone in this game and I was thankful she was with me at that time. We had to spend every minute together living like that and doing the same sort of work, so it wouldn't have worked if there wasn't a mutual respect and understanding, plus there was great support between us.

During the day we would either have photo shoots or castings. I'd turned 20 when we started to appear together more and more in *FHM*, *Loaded* and *Front* magazines, but, despite the regular work, the money we earned was still never enough. Normally we'd just save our pennies as best we could and we did manage to get by. Our work schedule consisted of beginning a day shoot at 10am. We would spend two hours in hair and make-up and four hours shooting. The make-up artists would always ask us what we wanted to look like, but because we were shooting 'glamour' the usual smoky eyes and glossy lips applied. Often we'd wear false eyelashes and get our nails painted and then we'd start the shoot. I always shot with Natalie or alone but I refused to shoot with men – I was shy and actually a bit of a prude, so to have been up close to and half-naked with a man I'd not met before would have been too uncomfortable for me.

Depending on the feature, we would either shoot on location in hotels or abroad, or in a London studio. Each shoot was different and each one was just as exciting as the first. Then, some evenings after work, Natalie and I would go out partying in the West End. We had a lot of contacts between us so getting invitations or on guest lists was never an issue. I'd been partying with Stacey for a good year by now and so I knew the ropes, where to go and who to meet up with. Any time there was a celebrity in town, Natalie and I would always be on the guest list. Whether our agent Yvonne arranged it or one of our contacts had called us, we were always there to see the night in. Because we were models and were now known faces, sometimes we just rocked up and the promoter or doorman would let us in, no questions asked. Stacey would sometimes join Natalie and I for nights out, but they didn't always see eye to eye.

Natalie

The only issue was, like I said, that we needed to watch our money. But, even then, we found a way to get round that! Being pretty models and a pair, drinks were bought for us wherever we went. We would share clothes and borrow them from other models. All we had to do was foot the cab bills to and from our bed-sit in Liverpool Street and show up for the night.

By 2003, Natalie and I had become professional party girls. After spending my first-ever night out at The Wellington with Stacey, it wasn't a surprise to me that that place became our focal point. I felt the most comfortable in there, mainly because the owner, Jake, and his staff always looked after us. As well as The Wellington being our specific little haunt, there was also a certain way that Natalie and I worked the London party circuit. In fact, we became real party professionals! When we got to know what party was happening that night, we would sit on our mattress in the bed-sit and plan what we were going to wear and would then share a bottle of wine while we got ready. We booked our cab and would head into the West End. The clubs we loved were Aura, Pangaea and Chinawhite. There were specific nights for each different club, and we would always be there. When we entered the club we would be invited to sit at tables with guys as soon as we came in through the door. Sometimes they would be men that we already knew, sometimes not, but they always had a lot of money and showered us with whatever we wanted. Often they just wanted female company but for them the main thing was to be seen sitting with us by other guys at other tables.

On the London club scene there was a huge ego thing

going on. As well as being seen with pretty girls, each table had to have more champagne than the other. If one table ordered a magnum of Cristal, then the one next to it would order two or three! The egomania would continue through the night and naturally the clubs, which would make thousands out of this ridiculous process, and party girls like Natalie and I would just have a great time. Funnily enough, I couldn't even tell you where these men were from or anything about them. We would spend hours chatting at a table with different men, but we rarely remembered anything about the conversations the next day. That was fair enough, but Natalie and I also placed ourselves in huge amounts of danger when we took the next step. Because there was free champagne flowing all night, often we would get quite tipsy and sometimes we didn't know where we were or who was with us at the end of a night. Looking back, I still can't believe I did the things I did.

One night was particularly dangerous. We had met a Middle Eastern guy, who was very handsome with thick dark hair, when we were out clubbing. We had joined his group at his table early on when we arrived at the club and, as usual, we were having a fantastic time. His friend liked Natalie and the other lads he was with were just there for the ride. We recognised their faces from a few weeks before so we felt comfortable drinking and dancing with them. But that night things went too far. The guy was giving me a lot of his champagne and as usual I accepted everything and carried on partying with him. He told me that he would tip the toilet attendant so that we could go into the cubicle together in the men's in case I wanted any cocaine. He was nice and polite, and I knew he had taken a shine to me, which was fine.

It was great having the attention, so, when his group wanted to carry on partying back at his place, we didn't think twice. 'We can go to my place,' he had said, smiling and stroking my hand. I knew what he wanted, but I was so out of it that I just thought about continuing the night and doing more cocaine. After all, Natalie was with me and as usual the drugs made me feel like everyone was my friend. We all hopped into a black cab and sped off. I remember the man's penthouse was stunning. The view through the huge glass windows was mesmerising but not as breathtaking as the van Gogh on the wall when we walked in! As we sat in the living room, I felt as if I was in another world. Taking a glass of champagne from the Middle Eastern man, I looked around in wonder.

'Can I show you something?' he suddenly whispered in my ear.

'Of course,' I replied before he ushered me into a bathroom next to the living room. He was soon chopping up more cocaine on the cabinet by the toilet; he rolled up a £50 note and handed it to me. But I had had so much to drink that I couldn't focus. I pushed the note away, but he then pushed me back. My reluctance didn't go down well and the man started to get heavy-handed. He gripped me tightly around the shoulders, forcing me up against the wall, and, as he shouted vile names at me, he started to push up my skirt. I was confused and disorientated, but as my mind started to settle I realised that I needed to find some strength to get him off. The trouble was that I was quite drunk that night, so my body wasn't functioning.

'You owe me! You need to repay me now, sweetheart,' he snarled, as I felt his fingers probing through my underwear.

'Please don't!' I cried and then whimpered, 'I can explain.'

But the more I tried to speak, the angrier he became. I slumped in his arms, but suddenly I heard Natalie pounding on the bathroom door. 'Are you all right, Cassie?' she screamed. 'Let me in! Let me in! I'm calling the police!'

The man quickly unlocked the door and sauntered out. Natalie ran in and pulled me up, shaking me violently. 'You've got to pull yourself together, Cassie,' she shouted. 'We need to get out of here now!' She left me on the floor and went to get our bags from the living room.

When she came back, I felt strong enough to walk and we ran as fast as we could out of the penthouse. After that night, I never saw the man or his friends again, but, despite the ferocity of that ordeal, it still didn't prevent me from hooking up with random guys again and going back to private after-parties with strangers. In the end, the risk never mattered because all I wanted to do at this point was party.

A few months later, we went back to another man's house, again after the clubs had shut, and with a group of men including a Greek guy, who had taken a shine to me. He was very good-looking, and he knew it, too, and I could tell that this might end in tears if we got on the wrong side of him. We sat around his dining-room table as he chopped up lines of thick chunky cocaine.

Suddenly I remembered what had happened the last time. 'I can't take this stuff,' I whispered to Natalie.

'Well, don't then,' she said, but before I could say anything else a huge row erupted.

'Get out, get out!' said the Greek man.

No one told him to be quiet so we felt incredibly vulnerable. We left and I remember turning around and looking up at his window with him shouting after us. It was almost dawn and there were Natalie and I roaming the streets in a really rough part of North London, wearing mini skirts and high heels. Both of us were still really drunk and I had taken cocaine so we were asking for trouble. We didn't even know how to get home and had no credit in our phones to call a cab so we stood on the edge of the road in the cold. Eventually we found a night bus and managed to scrape together enough change to get us both to Liverpool Street. I look back now and think how thankful I am that nothing ever happened to us on either of those occasions, but at the time partying had taken over my life and made me feel invincible.

Some mornings I'd wake up and cry because I was so embarrassed about the way I'd behaved the night before. I still cringe when I look back on incidents like the ones I've told you about, but I'm thankful I never got badly hurt and that eventually I learned from my mistakes. At the time, though, regardless of the mistakes I made, I was swept up in something so huge that, without my knowing it, my life had begun to spiral out of control.

Chapter Seven

Fun in the Sun

As well as partying hard and keeping up with the modelling, at this point I'd also discovered another avenue of pleasure. Although I was struggling financially, I was determined not to get another job on the side. I was 19 when I first heard about the lucrative world of hostessing. 'Loads of models do it, Cassie,' the model agent had said on the phone one morning. 'I can put you on our books straight away and you can earn as much as £1,000 per event.'

I jumped at the opportunity of getting involved because, as the women at one particular modelling agency had said, other models did it and it was a nice little earner. So, it was through this agency that I experienced my first-ever all-expenses paid trip on a luxurious private yacht on the swish Côte d'Azur in the summer of 2003. Sadly, it was this exclusive party abroad that later caused the press to question my status as a model, branding me an escort because of it. Quite frankly, to my mind at the time and even today, this just wasn't the case.

I remember receiving that first invitation to be a hostess. At the time I was living in Liverpool Street and, like I said, money was pretty tight. I didn't see anything underhand or sleazy about going away to party for a week for £1,000. 'We need three beautiful girls to hostess a party on a yacht in St Tropez,' the email stated.

After reading through the itinerary, I quickly called the model agent. 'Can you give me any more details?' I asked her, full of curiosity.

'It's simple. There are five men spending a week on a private yacht in the harbour in St Tropez. They're offering me £1,000 per girl just to party with them, nothing more. The money is yours if you want it, Cassie,' she explained.

I didn't even need to think. St Tropez, a fully crewed yacht, private quarters, exclusive nightclubs and sunshine, *and* I'd get paid, I thought bursting with excitement. 'When do you want me?' I asked her and the next weekend I was flying business class to Nice Airport with two other models.

I didn't know the other girls but during the flight we all got on fine. Helena was brunette and very sexy. She told me she'd hostessed many times before and mainly through the summer months; she highlighted the fact that she couldn't make ends meet as a glamour model and these parties enabled her to have a holiday and to network. 'It's fine, Cassie. You'll love it. You get looked after impeccably. There's never any trouble. You get to network and there are so many incredible celebrities in St Tropez at this time of year,' she smiled.

Fun in the Sun

The other model, Nicola, was blonde and curvy. Like me, it was her first trip so I was glad there was another novice.

When we landed at Nice, we were ushered towards a blacked-out limousine. A chauffeur hopped out of the front and opened the door for us. 'Help yourself to champagne and we'll be in St Tropez in half an hour,' he said in a heavy French accent.

I climbed in after the other two girls and the three of us sipped champagne and chatted happily all the way there. I had no idea what to expect, but, when we pulled into the harbour and were shown our yacht, I couldn't believe my eyes. It was incredible! There, on the water in all its glory, it was huge and inviting!

I then spotted a dark-haired man standing on the sun deck. Four other men, all of whom looked Arabic, surrounded him. 'Welcome aboard!' he shouted. He'd seen us standing at the foot of the gangplank and was waving us over.

I was wearing high heels and it was hard tottering up the wood on to the sun deck, but, when Hassan introduced himself, he made me feel so relaxed and welcome. He was short and well built, with a warm, friendly face.

'Come, girls, I'll show you to your rooms,' he said. 'Then we'll have champagne and canapés on the deck before dinner.'

We all traipsed into the inner deck area and looked around. The yacht was decked out in an amazing Versace décor. Everywhere, there were cream carpets and soft pale-blue walls. There were several stunning bedrooms, which were light and airy, with mirrored walls and modern furniture. Hassan showed me the room I was to share with Helena.

'There are staff on board and they will tend to your every need. There is a hair salon at the back of the yacht and we can supply a beautician whenever you feel the need,' he explained. 'I'll leave you all to unpack and freshen up, then do come and join me on the sun deck. We need to get to know one another.' Hassan seemed kind and endearing enough, so I felt glad that I'd made the trip.

That night we put on our cocktail dresses and enjoyed champagne and caviar with the five men, followed by an exquisite four-course dinner by candlelight. We chatted about London and our jobs as models and the men told us they were businessmen from Dubai. They were in the oil business so it was obvious they had huge incomes, and, despite our different cultures and incomes, they were all charming to us. Our little group was in great spirits when we finally headed into the centre of St Tropez to an amazing club called Jimmy's. Because the club was located outside, the atmosphere in Jimmy's was awesome: wall-to-wall models and rich good-looking men were sipping Champagne Bellinis and cocktails. Hassan knew most of the guests in the VIP area and I was introduced to oil barons, traders and multi-millionaire shipping magnates. Despite the amount of money that was there, everyone was incredibly polite and friendly just like the men with whom we were staying on the yacht. I had a fantastic night and rolled into bed tipsy at 3am.

The next day I woke to the sound of the sea lapping against the side of the yacht. This is bliss, I thought and leaped up happily to start the day. We'd been told we could please ourselves until the evening and so we got dressed and ate breakfast together, then decided to head to a favourite celebrity haunt that Helena had been to before called Nikki Beach. I put on my sexiest bikini and new Dior sunglasses and we all wandered over to where the beach started. Inside the entrance barriers I could see loads of tanned and toned people stretched out happily on the bright-yellow sun loungers. I could hear a bar pumping out music on the far side. 'Let's go and get a drink,' I suggested to the other girls and, as we approached the crowded bar, I noticed Puff Daddy and Cindy Crawford enjoying cocktails at different tables. They were laughing and chatting with their respective groups. Puff Daddy was surrounded by bikini-clad girls and seemed to be having the time of his life. I wondered if the girls were friends or hostesses like us, but, regardless of what Puffy was up to, I was in complete paradise that afternoon. I even spotted Pamela Anderson the next afternoon and partied with Puff Daddy the following one. He was so friendly and polite, not like I'd imagined at all!

As the week progressed, we got ourselves into a nice little routine. After breakfast we'd head to Nikki Beach to sunbathe and party with the stars and then during the evenings we'd spend time dining with the men on the yacht. Most nights we'd end up at Jimmy's or I'd get an early night. I wasn't sure at the start of the week, but there wasn't anything seedy about them at all because all they wanted was the company of pretty girls. Because I'd hit it off with Hassan, we swapped numbers on the day we left. 'I'll call you when I'm in London,' he said, smiling. 'I'll need a night out when I get there and it would be great if you could organise a table somewhere special and bring some of your friends.'

'Of course,' I replied, and as we left the yacht I really looked forward to our next meeting. Hassan had given me a taste of such an amazing lifestyle that I'd never dreamed existed, but I also enjoyed making a new friend.

It was a month later when he finally called. 'It will be great to see you tonight, Cassie. I'd love to try out Pangaea and meet some of your friends,' he said excitedly on the phone. 'I'm only here in London on business until tomorrow.'

I spent the day booking a VIP table for him at the club and then arranged for a few of my girlfriends to join us. I didn't expect anything from him because Hassan was a friend, but, when we got to the club, he slipped an envelope in my hand. 'This is for all the hard work you've done for me today, Cassie. Treat yourself. I know it's hard for you on a model's wage.'

And so it became a regular thing for Hassan to hand over £1,000 whenever he came into town. It only happened a handful of times, but I didn't see any problem with it. I knew that £1,000 was peanuts to him and he valued me as a friend. Later, I found out that he was a prince and that he often got lonely. I respected Hassan because he never laid a finger on me or any of my friends; and I was always relaxed and open with him because our relationship wasn't about sex at all. For him, it was about spending time with beautiful young women and for me it was like getting a taste of paradise. After the third or fourth time, Hassan stopped calling but I assume that perhaps he'd got married.

As for the hostessing, another opportunity like St Tropez came up, but at the time I was busy. Stacey eventually warned me how working as a hostess while trying to cut it as a model might affect my profile in the future. 'You need to be careful with that side of the scene, Cassie,' she said one night when I'd told her about the trip. 'If you want to be taken seriously as a glamour model and move on to bigger things, then you shouldn't get involved in hostess work. They'll label you an escort for doing it. If the press get wind of it, you'll regret it, especially if you become more famous.'

When I listened to what she said, I thought that perhaps I'd been naive to think that anyone outside my industry might look on hostessing differently, but I really didn't think being a hostess would make any difference to my career because I wasn't doing anything wrong. In the end I told the modelling agency that got the hostessing work for me to take me off their books for fear of it affecting my career – and then I forgot about it.

Later on, when I was filming *WAGs Boutique*, the press did find out about this part of my life but, just as Stacey had said, they completely distorted it and labelled me an escort. In my mind back then, and even now, I was a hostess on a yacht. I had an amazing time as I partied with a few men and a week later I left the yacht and kept up with a friend I'd made along the way. There wasn't anything seedy or underhand about it then and there isn't now, which is why I've been open and honest about it. I've nothing to hide, but, as is often the way of the media, they like to think I have.

Hopefully, other models tempted to hostess will take

heed and opt for another path because of what happened to me. Had someone in the industry warned me about how the media might portray hostessing, or how hostessing might have a negative impact on my career before I did it, then I definitely wouldn't have done it. If Stacey hadn't warned me after that first trip, then I might have hostessed a lot more than I did and I might not be in the position I am now to be able to tell the truth.

Chapter Eight

Cocaine Nights

BACK IN LONDON, THINGS CHANGED SO QUICKLY AFTER
NATALIE AND I STARTED TO HIT THE PARTY SCENE. I was 20
and within six months we'd already moved to a new flat
and it really felt as if we were finally making something of
our lives.

I remember the morning when Natalie and I unpacked
our bags at our brand-new flat, which was above The
Wellington club. 'Thank goodness for Jake,' I'd said to
her, as we sat happily together in the smart bedroom of the
plush Knightsbridge penthouse.

'I know,' she replied. 'I couldn't take that awful place
any longer. Jake has given us a fresh start. We can really
focus on partying now, Cassie. We needed to network
more and now look what's happened: we're living above
the hippest club in town!'

We knew we owed Jake a great deal after we moved into
his top-floor apartment above The Wellington.

Jake came into our lives because we'd started partying at his club every night. He was warm, kind and funny, and we adored him from the moment he approached us at the bar. Jake was older, but still good-looking with his tan and greyish hair. Because we clicked and he knew that Natalie and I were the two 'new girls on the block', he kindly took us under his wing. 'Why don't you both stay in one of the bedrooms at the penthouse upstairs for a while?' he said one evening as he handed us each another glass of Cristal. 'You're in the club most nights, so it'll be convenient and safer for you. I know you're struggling over where you are in Liverpool Street. You could look after the place for me in return and then come down to the club as much as you like to network and that would be great for your profiles and also keep my punters happy.'

Natalie and I sipped our champagne and glanced at each other knowingly. For both of us, Jake's words felt like a blessing. We were sick and tired of the bed-sit and, because we seemed to be spending most of our time out networking, we really weren't doing enough modelling work to pay the rent. If we moved into Jake's penthouse, it would mean less outgoings for us and we could socialise in his club whenever we liked. This was the perfect opportunity. I remember standing in front of Jake and swallowing the cool bubbly liquid. 'Natalie and I would love to move in, Jake. Name your day,' I said.

I'd moved to London when I was just 19, but sadly, by the age of 20, I was taking more cocaine. I do feel guilty and upset about this part of my life because I made a mistake during this time and I also lost my way. I just wish someone had been there for me to help and warn me of what dangers lay ahead. Sadly, I almost lost touch with my modelling dream. I'd tried the drug a few times before, but sniffing cheap coke off a broken toilet seat while huddled in a grubby pub toilet didn't have the same appeal as taking it in an exclusive London nightclub. Cocaine on the London scene was a totally different ballgame. Taking it in luxurious, opulent surroundings while listening to stylish music and having beautiful people whispering in my ear made the experience feel really magical.

Now that we were living upstairs in the penthouse and everyone knew me, we started throwing after-parties. When the club shut, it was much safer and more glamorous partying in the privacy of my own penthouse living room. 'Are you joining us tonight upstairs?' I would say to whoever Natalie and I were partying with that particular night in the club.

Whenever we threw a party upstairs, there was always plenty of coke around to make the party go with a swing. I'd look out through the floor-to-ceiling windows in front of me and see the whole of Knightsbridge in all its splendour, and then, over to the left, the depressing buildings of Liverpool Street. I always felt amazing, sitting there and thinking how far I'd come. Natalie and I would then sit together, looking at the stunning view and talking about nothing well into the small hours. At this point I felt great about my life. I lived in a beautiful area where all the beautiful parties were being held. I felt safe being around friends, who I thought cared about me and I felt that I belonged.

Sometimes even when I wasn't partying with my new

friends in the living room, I'd often wake up in the middle of the night to hear people chatting outside my bedroom. I would get up, clean my teeth and head half-asleep into the living room; I would do a line with whoever was there and spend the next few hours talking with them until the sun came up. Then, some mornings I'd wake up and there would be people still taking cocaine in the living room. 'Here, Cassie, have a line,' the partygoers would sometimes say to me, smiling, and often I would join them for a line as my breakfast. It didn't bother me at the time but looking back I was definitely starting to take too much.

At the time, there was another girl living in the penthouse with us called Tintin. She wasn't a model but worked downstairs in the club every night. A family friend of Jake's, she would help him out with booking the tables and arranging his guest lists. Tintin knew everyone because she came into contact with new people every night and it was her job to be friendly and welcoming to them. She was very popular and had friends in fashion, music and the city. Because she liked me, she happily introduced me to everyone she knew and so my network of contacts began to expand quickly. As my party network started to grow, so did the number of invitations I got and gradually the parties all rolled into one. Unfortunately, none of that helped me to stop taking drugs.

As I explained earlier, at the beginning of my life in London, the amount of drugs available to a partygoer had shocked me. Over time I discovered that, if you weren't offered cocaine at the door of a private party, there would be piles of it on the sideboards or on tables in other rooms. People would either scoop up the drug as they wished or take it in the bathrooms. Sometimes there were other drugs available, though I often didn't know what they were.

One night, I'd gone to a penthouse party in Battersea, South London. Natalie and I had been told that it was *the* place to be in London that night so we were filled with excitement when we got the invite. A City boy we met two weeks earlier had invited us and had called us that afternoon telling us we *had* to make it. When we walked out of the lift, we entered the main room. There were circus people doing acts in front of us and a huge sound system pumped out house music over a massive floodlit bar. We wandered around and noticed that each room had its own bar and waiting staff. It was swarming with City people and celebrities – or what we then knew to be the London rich set.

Within minutes I was offered cocaine. 'The drinks are over there, the drugs are in that room and of course help yourself to cigarettes,' said the tall, slender woman obviously hosting the party. 'I'm glad you two could make it,' she smiled, licking her thick red glossy lips. She didn't know us, but by then I knew that cocaine made everyone friends.

'Thanks,' I said, and wandered off, leaving Natalie in the living room.

It was that night in the Battersea penthouse that I learned the hard way. 'Try some of this, Cassie,' said the dark-haired pop star as he stood next to me by the huge mirrored table. He was famous for his boyish looks, being in a one-time successful boy band but he was also a known user on the circuit. I looked at the white powder he'd carefully chopped up for me on the table. It was sitting there, waiting for me in a thin perfectly formed line.

Already I'd drunk a lot of champagne and, as often happened when I felt slightly drunk, I couldn't resist the temptation. I inserted a rolled-up £50 note in my right nostril and inhaled deeply. The drug shot through my nose, straight into my head. But the usual buzz I felt whenever I sniffed coke didn't happen. 'What was that?' I asked the pop star. Already I was slurring my words.

'Just a bump of Ketamine,' he said. 'You'll love it, Cassie, don't worry!'

Ketamine, or 'K' as it is known, is a horse tranquilliser and if you take it with cocaine it gives you a balanced feeling of control. It's called CK on the party scene and is very common. You can experience the high from the cocaine, neutralised with the Ketamine, and that sensation is supposed to be fantastic. That particular night I thought I was sniffing cocaine, but then I started to act strangely. I didn't actually care what the man was saying to me about the drug because I couldn't even stand up. My legs felt solid and my mind went completely blank. I felt as if I wasn't in my own body at all and that I needed to sit down. 'Here, drink this,' he said, handing me a glass of water. But I couldn't even lift the glass; it felt like a lead weight in my hand. In the end the man had to help me drink it and when I sat down I had to stay there with him until the drug had worn off. It was a horrible start to the night because I felt scared and foolish. In the end, I left the party early and as I headed home I promised myself to be more careful next time. I needed to keep my head together in case I made a mistake again.

It wasn't long before I witnessed other highly addictive drugs being taken on the scene and those memories have never faded. One night we'd been partying at a DJ's house since the night before. No one slept or ate, everyone just partied. On this occasion, the drug-taking around me was really quite extraordinary. The party ran out of cocaine and so the DJ wanted to order some more. 'Can you bring some crack over soon?' he asked on his mobile. 'As soon as possible.' I remember his voice was tinged with panic.

Fifteen minutes later, the doorbell rang. The DJ came back into the living room with a small package. He sat down and pulled out a small glass pipe. He lit the end of the pipe and proceeded to smoke it before offering the pipe to the other people, who were sitting wide-eyed next to him. When he offered it to me, I declined quickly, and turned and walked into the kitchen.

I knew that I had an addictive streak in me at that point in my life, but I'm lucky I didn't smoke the crack because I knew it could be even more addictive. As I stood in the kitchen I remembered the Ketamine I'd mistakenly taken a month beforehand. It was disgusting to have watched that scene unfold in front of me but the saddest thing was that to them it was just another drug. Unfortunately, that wasn't the end for this particular crowd. The crack ran out and, because they were all so wasted, the DJ rang up the dealer again and as I stood alone in the kitchen I overheard him ordering heroin. At that point, I'd started to feel tired so I wandered into a nearby bedroom and fell asleep.

A few hours later, because I'd woken up, I went back into the living room. The party had emptied out apart from a few who were now slumped on the sofa. A needle was on the coffee table and as I looked at their pale, sallow faces I could see their eyes rolling and yellow. It was a revolting sight and it shocked me to the core because they had obviously moved on to heroin. I had to get out, so I quickly called a taxi and left. As I stood in the cold, waiting for the cab to arrive, I was so distraught. I knew and socialised with people who took crack and heroin: they were household names; they had decent jobs and were respected in the industry. Remembering that night still disturbs me to this day.

I never saw that crowd together again, even though I often saw those famous faces out partying after that. But for me, regardless of the heroin and crack that I'd seen being taken, I was still taking too much cocaine myself. Just to give you an idea, I often partied through the night, sometimes going through to the next one. Sometimes I stayed awake for three days at a time. I can't even say how much cocaine I would have needed to keep me awake during those hours, but it was a lot, perhaps eight or nine grams in a week.

At the time I was young so I didn't worry about my looks. I was 21 and was having the time of my life. I didn't think about eating or getting old because I just lived for the day. Sure, I went to some amazing parties and at the time it felt like everything to me. Money was tight because I wasn't modelling that much but nothing mattered because I was enjoying myself so much and was wanted by everyone at his or her fabulously extravagant party. It made me feel important and that I was finally worth something; mixing with such high-flying people gave me a false sense of security.

When you are partying with A-list stars and celebrities, it really gets to you. Natalie and I would party with any

A-lister who happened to be in town. One weekend we'd be enjoying champagne with Eminem in Chinawhite and the next sipping cocktails at an after-party with 50 Cent.

The Pharrell Williams party we went to was the best. We'd been at Chinawhite and were invited back to an amazing townhouse for the after-party. It was a very exclusive party and only the best people were allowed in. 'I want you and Cassie there,' the host had said as Natalie and I were leaving the club that night. This man was very selective with his friends and whom he invited to his parties, so, if he called on you, you knew you were with the 'in' crowd. I remember his Mayfair house was hidden away like a hotel in a quiet street off Green Park. As we approached in the black cab, I could see the courtyard was packed with Ferraris, Bentleys and Ducati motorbikes. I clambered out of the cab and went over to the huge black front door. Security cameras were panning down on us and we had to ring the buzzer and say our names before we were let in.

When I got inside, I really felt like I was the luckiest girl alive. There were waitresses galore, wearing tiny silver outfits trimmed with sequins and pearls. They sauntered around with silver trays, offering guests whatever they wanted. Smartly dressed waiters lined the huge marble staircase, which swooped into a huge candle-lit reception area where the partygoers were having the time of their lives. And I was, too! I'm so lucky to be here. I'm going to party hard tonight. It's Pharrell's party and I've been invited, I thought. I knew I was at this amazing party with all the right people and I thought that, if I met someone special, it would really help my profile. But, like every other party I'd been to, I just got swept up in the moment. It wasn't really about my profile because being at a party like that one and mixing with those people made me feel wanted and it filled the void.

That night I partied all night. I sat with Pharrell and we talked about New York and London; we talked about partying and films. I really thought he was my best friend. But Pharrell or no Pharrell, I was in complete denial. The truth was that, if there was a party I could go to, that would take precedence over work. In the end, it wasn't about Pharrell or the modelling work: it was all about partying and getting high. I'd started to live my life just so that I could go out. I used to say to myself, 'It's fine; I'm young so I can do this now. I can live my life now and when I'm older I'll stop partying!' I even got a tattoo etched on my neck, which said 'Carpe Diem'. That's what I did; I lived for the moment and didn't worry about the future or the past, but I was just fooling myself because I was just running away from the feelings I had about Papa and I was too scared to face the future because I'd lost touch with my modelling dream along the way. I used partying and the drugs as a way of escaping from the harsh reality of life and from my past troubles – to me, it felt easier than having to face my issues head on.

If I was ever working I'd stay awake through the job and would often drop diet pills to keep me awake. The diet pill I took was called Effedrin, which is an amphetamine. Sometimes I would carry on partying after work. I would have a photo shoot and, because my hair and make-up was done, that was a bonus and it gave me an excuse to go out that night. This really should have been a point in

Above left: Happy days. Mum and Papa at their wedding.

Above right: Water baby – I loved sun and water from an early age. Here I am in the pool with Mum.

Below left: Me and my brother, Ben, having fun with Papa on the beach in Menorca.

Below right: Even at five years old, I was fashion conscious. My red wellies finish off the outfit nicely.

ST. EDWARD'S R.C. PRIMARY SCHOOL

Name _Cassie Munoz_

Class _2_

Report Year Ending _1989_

Attendance _Good._

GRADES

Mathematics		English		Reading		Reading Comprehension		Science & Technology

Subject	Effort	Comment	Subject	Effort	Comment
Language Development & Communication		Still very quiet and a little shy. Communicates adequately one-to-one.	Science Concepts		Participates well in group-based activities & shows interest
Reading		Very slow progress. Frequently mislays book.	Social Attitude		Quiet well-behaved. Friendly & popular.
Mathematics		Steady progress. Cassie tries hard with her number work. Quite promising.	Physical Education		Not overly keen on P.E.
Writing	Creative	Very keen to succeed & willing to work hard. Skills are improving.	Creative Activities		Enjoys art & craft activities - produces lovely pictures. Very neat & careful worker. Shows promise
	Skills	neat handwriting - room for improvement - gradually getting better.	Project based work		

Class Teacher: _Cassie tries hard to please "Miss". She still seems very young for her age. Quite a good effort overall._

R. Spruce

Headteacher: _Immature Cassie needs to grow in confidence_ _S. O'Hagan_

Above: When Mum married Patrick, not only were we lucky enough to have him as part of our family but we also gained a new brother and sister, Megan and Conor.

Below: My school report. Although I was a bit of a loner at school, I adored art and still love making things today.

Above: Wedding bells for Mum and Patrick – and flower girl duties for me!

Below left: I'm not sure if Ben and I were taking Scruffy for a walk, or if he was taking us!

Below right: Conor and Megan when they were teenagers.

Starting out – one of my very first test shots as a model.

Above: Christmas belles. (*From left to right*) Donatella, Sam, me and Nicola.

Below left: With my best friend, Stacey.

Below right: Fun in the sun – relaxing with (*from left to right*) Gemma, Dani and another Gemma!

Glamour girl! Once I got started, I loved doing photo shoots and soon got over any initial nerves.

When I met Celestine, I was at a really low point. He helped me to get back on my feet.

© *Offsid*

my life when I was happy 24/7. On the outside it looked like I had come so far: I was living in an amazingly luxurious flat in the most exclusive area of London; I was a model and was attending the most prestigious of parties, but the depression that I felt inside when I left Sheppey had returned. It was obvious why and I knew full well what was going on, but I just chose to ignore it.

The comedowns started to get worse just because trying to chase those highs was getting even harder. I would see amazing things at amazing parties and experience amazing feelings of euphoria. The problem was that they were never, ever the same as the first time. When you first start taking cocaine you don't need much, maybe a few lines in a night, but, when you take more, you can end up needing two or three grams to get to where you want to again. I had no recollection of days, dates or time, and to this day people often approach me when I'm out and say, 'Cassie, do you remember me?' But I can't for the life of me place their faces. All I feel when this happens is regret and fear. I fear what I might have said to someone if I was drunk or high, or how I might have acted. I regret that I must have missed a massive chunk of my life, which to this day often comes back to haunt me.

Sadly, the people I do remember I have lost along the way because they are still doing what I did back then. They never moved on, and it's harsh to say but I do find it all a bit pathetic now and am so glad that I finally wised up. Because I was so addicted to partying, which in turn took me to the depths of despair, I would never take it to that extreme again. And when I say extreme, I mean it. I know that I partied for days and days, drinking and taking coke.

Once I sniffed a gram in half an hour. I was showing off at the time but it just showed how much I could take. I would only worry when I was at home in bed and feeling tired after a party. I'd be on a comedown and would have to take valium to knock myself out otherwise I'd be suicidal.

The crippling moments when I started to feel suicidal were the worst. 'What are you doing to yourself?' the shrill voice would often shriek in my head. I'd turn over in bed, trying to turn it off. The drug-taking had got so bad that I was hearing negative voices in my head but it was my own voice of reason battling the drugs. When I lay in bed after a heavy session and my body was 'clucking' (an expression which refers to an intense craving for more drugs), I'd think over and over about partying, taking cocaine and wishing I hadn't become a part of this life. If there had been a gun in the drawer next to my bed, then I would take it out and shoot myself, I thought many a time.

Once I was at my friend Tim's house and yet again it was a morning where I was trying to sleep. He lived in North London and I would often party there with him. I remember looking over at Tim, who was lying next to me, sleeping soundly. I couldn't wake him up to talk to him in case he thought I was being weak. Then I thought, if I did anything silly, Tim might get in trouble, and so that morning, just like all the others, I reached for the bottle of valium stashed away in my make-up bag and knocked myself out.

Taking as many drugs as I was taking at this time in my life can have serious consequences in the future. It's definitely had a long-term effect on me and I suffer from mood swings and really bad bouts of depression. My short-term memory is now also poor and I suffer from paranoia. However much fun people think they are having at the time, this kind of drug use just isn't worth the long-term health risks.

I knew full well when I thought about suicide that it was a vicious circle: because I normally felt so bad, the next day I always got back on the cocaine. As I entered my 21st year and the partying continued to get out of hand, so did my journey into the sleazy London underworld, where my next encounter was way too much for me. I continued to make mistakes, but there always comes a point where things go too far.

Chapter Nine

The Madam

I THOUGHT I'D SEEN IT ALL AFTER I'D BEEN OFFERED CRACK WHEN I WAS OUT PARTYING, BUT EVEN THAT NASTY EXPERIENCE DIDN'T DETER ME FROM MIXING IN THOSE CROWDS. For me, the appeal of partying was still there and I still felt the need to belong; I just didn't know what I was doing by that point. The money, the drugs and the people made me feel special and a part of something so extremely exclusive. I was totally wrapped up in this new world, where I felt I'd found a place. I thought that if I didn't go out and party I'd feel lost and alone, like I'd done in the past. I'd also failed to find a sense of lasting worth as a model, so embraced the lifestyle wholeheartedly.

It was a month or so after I turned 21 when I came into full contact with another decadent part of the London party scene, but the most difficult thing that I had to deal with was that I became unknowingly involved. Escorting wasn't something I knowingly chose to encounter and I knew I'd never again make a mistake like the one I made the night that I was duped. I still remember being in a very bad frame of mind when it came into my life, so I can understand now why it happened and why I didn't deal with it appropriately. 'Have I got any shoots or castings on this week?' I'd ask Yvonne most Monday mornings. I was normally very hungover from a full night of Sunday-night partying so didn't actually care about her answer.

'Sorry, love, it's really quiet,' she would say and the line would go dead.

Part of me always felt relieved that Yvonne still wasn't coming up with jobs for me, because not having any modelling assignments meant that I could go back to bed after the phone call and party again that night. Partying took my mind off work and it took my mind off the lack of money in my life. It was strange to think that I had initially thrown myself into partying to get noticed as a model, but, because that hadn't paid off, I was now partying for other reasons. Partying was like a drug and I'd got so wrapped up in it all that nothing else mattered apart from reaching that high. The difficulty was that I found myself increasingly struggling because of it.

One night my curiosity about the wealth that I constantly saw around me started to intensify. Suddenly I felt different from everyone around me and frustrated with my frugal lifestyle as I stood at the bar in The Wellington and looked around the club. It was yet another night where I was wearing a Top Shop dress that I'd worn on the same night the week beforehand and, yet again, I couldn't buy any drinks either. But there I was in an exclusive nightclub, surrounded by sheer luxury. It was a huge contradiction but it had never bothered me so much as it did then. I always wondered what the other girls did for work and how they juggled partying and their careers because they obviously had money. I knew these girls: they always had coke and drank Cristal – I couldn't figure out how they were so rich.

The men chatting animatedly next to me were dressed head to toe in Prada and Gucci; their bar bill was heading into the thousands already. I spotted a group of young beautiful women standing over by the VIP area. They were draped in Dior and Versace. I imagined their handbags would be overflowing with cocaine. I looked at their shoes and, sure enough, they were the most expensive of brands. When these women leave the club tonight they will hop into their chauffeur-driven car or their boyfriend's Bentley and drive to their Park Lane penthouse. They probably order as much cocaine as they want when they get home and then spend the next day happily relaxing in bed, I told myself that night.

I realised their fantastically luxurious lifestyle was so extremely different from mine, but, like me, all they did was party at the club. That night I thought that I needed to find the key: if they can have this lifestyle and be able to afford it, then I also needed to find out how I can, I told myself at the bar. Then I noticed a woman in the club, who was a regular; she always sat regally in the same corner. She was just like the women I'd seen at the VIP tables, but she had this aura about her that made her seem invincible. It was as if she had power over everyone who approached or even looked at her, and, even before that night, I'd often wondered who she was. When I stood at the bar with Natalie, I would watch her sometimes and I often wanted to be like her – I wanted that power, grace, confidence and sex appeal, but I also wanted the money she seemed to have.

She was tall and busty with long dark hair. I could tell that she was on cocaine and she was dripping in diamonds. She wore Roberto Cavalli dresses and expensive watches, plus she was always with different guys, who also looked very rich. Every night, she would party with Chelsea footballers and she was also friends with other glamour models.

That night I thought that perhaps this woman held the key to getting the lifestyle that I craved. She looked particularly radiant and was swamped by gorgeous, expensively dressed, sexy men. Maybe it was because I wanted her to see me that I stared so much, but suddenly she waved me over and gestured for me to sit next to her at her table. I'll call her Jasmine to preserve her identity. 'What's your name, darling?' she murmured.

'It's Cassie,' I replied shyly, sitting down after she'd patted the seat next to her and offered me a glass of champagne.

Her hands were dainty and perfectly manicured. Each nail was painted in an expensive glossy red varnish. Her dress was black satin and perfectly accentuated her stunning figure. I was immediately in awe of this woman.

As we chatted, however, I realised she did have connections and money but I didn't feel comfortable about asking her what she did. I was just happy to be sitting with someone I was so in awe of.

We'd been drinking champagne for a few hours and she

handed me a wrap under the table. 'Do you want a line?' she asked me quietly.

'No thanks, Jasmine,' I replied and took another sip of champagne. I didn't want any cocaine that night and so I looked the other way. Then I noticed one of the men at the table staring at me.

'Would you like anything else, darling?' he asked.

'I'm fine for now, thanks,' I replied.

'What about *anything else* in the world?' said Jasmine, laughing and fixing her gaze on my lips.

'What do you mean?' I asked.

'Hamid says you can have anything you like in the world!' she said with a grin.

At first, I didn't understand what she meant and was just flattered that the dark-haired, handsome man who seemed to like me was being so generous!

The next moment Hamid moved round the table to sit next to me. He pressed his hand on mine and said, 'Let's get some more Cristal and then you choose which club you want to go to next.'

Hamid was incredibly good-looking with intense dark eyes; he was well groomed and smelled fantastic. He seemed so kind and nice and I warmed to him straight away.

'Cassie, you know you can have whatever you wish for tonight,' he repeated over and over to me as we sat close to one another. He then telephoned a particular night-club because I'd mentioned that I would have quite like to go there.

When the best table at the club had been booked, Jasmine, another man, Hamid and I all gulped down the rest of the champagne he'd bought and clambered into a waiting car.

When we got to the club it was packed. Hamid's security guard ushered us in and we were seated at the first table in the club's exclusive VIP area. I felt like a princess as Hamid tended to my every need. If I wanted cocaine or champagne, I know I could have had it within seconds; if I needed to go to the ladies' room, his security man would escort me. This is a different ballgame, I thought, as I reapplied my lipstick there. This man is something else. And then I realised that Jasmine was the one who held the key to what I wanted. She knew the best people and, like Hamid, she was making me feel special. I wanted to be like her and to able to be a part of her rich crowd; I wanted whatever she had, and I wanted it now, I thought to myself as I snapped my handbag shut and waltzed back to the VIP table.

I was really attracted to Hamid and I knew he liked me. He was devastatingly good-looking and so charming; I couldn't believe this was happening to me. A few hours earlier I'd been standing glumly at the bar in The Wellington feeling sorry for myself and, now, here I was with Jasmine and an amazing man, who was offering me anything I wanted in the world! When I sat back down, Hamid clicked his fingers at his security guard, who ushered us quickly out of the club and into the waiting Bentley.

'Are we going to yours, darling?' asked Jasmine.

'Sure,' Hamid replied, as we sped off into the night.

But I felt safe with these three people in the back of the Bentley and thought they were my friends. I then felt Jasmine clasp my hand. 'Don't worry, darling,' she whispered next to me, smiling. 'You'll have the night of your life tonight.'

We arrived at a quaint mews house and entered through

a back door. There were security guards everywhere and a camera device in every corner of every room. Although the house was small, there were three storeys and everything was controlled by remote. I'd noticed in the club that Hamid could even see his security cameras on his mobile phone; it was all so out of this world. He took my hand and we wandered up the first flight of stairs together. We then sat down in the open-plan living room and Hamid emptied a huge bag of cocaine on to the coffee table. I looked at the drugs and then looked up at him. I was massively attracted to him, but I'd started to feel unwell. It was getting late and I was feeling quite shaky from all the excitement and the champagne. 'I think I need to go home,' I murmured softly. 'I'm really sorry, but I have had too much to drink.'

Hamid looked upset, but he didn't say anything.

'I'll call you a cab, darling,' Jasmine said quickly.

When the cab arrived, I kissed Hamid goodbye and we agreed to see one another again. On arriving back at the penthouse, I fell into my bed, feeling happier than ever: I'd made some new friends who had money and an amazing lifestyle that I aspired to and they wanted to be *my* friends! Hamid wanted 'me' and he was from this world; it all seemed such perfect timing.

The next day it was early when Jasmine called. 'Hamid wants to see you tonight!' she laughed down the phone.

My heart skipped a beat. 'Definitely! But I'm so hungover after last night. Tell him to call me any time today to arrange,' I said.

'He's busy today, Cassie. He's very high profile so you need to be discreet and do as I say. What you need to do is get yourself to the gym, have a sauna and steam, get your hair and nails done and be ready for 8pm. Wear something sexy and black. Hamid will pick you up,' Jasmine said and hung up.

It felt like I was going to an interview but I was over the moon that Hamid wanted to see me again. I thought it was strange that he hadn't called me himself to ask me to go out with him, but excitement got the better of me and I didn't actually care. Soon I was putting myself through a rigorous workout session in the gym and imagining marriage and kids and love! It all seemed too perfect because Hamid was in his early thirties and was dashing, plus he'd asked me out straight away.

At 8pm on the dot, a big blacked-out Bentley arrived outside The Wellington. I'd prepared myself well and was wearing a black satin dress and a cute pair of heels. I felt a huge buzz of excitement when the chauffeur opened the car door for me. Hamid wasn't waiting for me inside, which was disappointing, but, as I sat back and relaxed on the pristine black leather seats, my mobile rang. 'It's Hamid, sweetheart. Would you like to pick a restaurant?' he said softly.

'Oh, gosh, um, OK, how about San Lorenzo's?' I replied. San Lorenzo's was my favourite restaurant in London, but I hadn't had the money to eat there in months.

'Done!' he said. 'I'll see you there in ten minutes.'

My heart fluttered. This is amazing for a first date, I thought to myself. Hamid is really trying to impress me. And he did impress me when I spotted him waiting patiently outside the restaurant.

'You look beautiful, Cassie,' he said, kissing me softly on both cheeks.

The Madam

I couldn't get my words out because he looked so dazzling and smelled delicious. We sat down at a quiet table at the back of the restaurant. It felt so intimate as Hamid ordered champagne and caviar to share. 'You order whatever you like for your main course,' he said.

I knew the menu and chose my favourite, which was Lobster Ravioli.

The champagne flowed throughout the meal and I relaxed into the conversation as he talked to me about his home country and I told him about the difficulties I'd encountered on the modelling scene. Enamoured by him, I didn't want the night to end and so, when the bill came, I was happy when he suggested that we should continue our night at a casino.

When we got to the casino it was buzzing. Suited men with expensively dressed girls draped on their arms were throwing chips on to the tables. Hand in hand, we walked to one of the Black Jack tables and Hamid taught me how to play. When he bought me lots of chips to gamble with, I really felt he cared whether or not I was having fun. I ordered a glass of water because I was slightly giddy from all the champagne and didn't want to make a fool of myself.

'Will you come back to my hotel?' Hamid whispered affectionately in my ear.

I didn't even have to think about it because I was having such a nice time and suddenly I wanted to go somewhere quiet with him; I didn't question why he mentioned a hotel instead of his mews house, so I agreed and we ended up at The Lanesborough in one of their top-floor penthouse suites.

Inside, I sat down on the king-sized bed and we started kissing. His kisses were soft and tender and after he'd undressed me we were soon having sex. It was totally fantastic and I fell asleep afterwards feeling amazing.

The next morning I remember waking up and feeling disorientated. I remembered the night before, the fantastic dinner and the mind-blowing sex we'd enjoyed in the luxurious hotel suite. I looked around the room because Hamid wasn't there in the bed next to me. I then heard the sound of water running in the bathroom, where he must have been taking a shower. I looked at the clock on the table next to me: it was 8am. My head was pounding from the alcohol, but as I started to get out of the bed Hamid emerged from the bathroom wearing a towel. 'Your money is on the table in the next room,' he said curtly, as he dried himself off with the towel.

'Thanks,' I replied and then murmured softly, 'Why don't you come back to bed?'

It was nice of him to pay for my taxi, but, when he didn't reply, I felt something was wrong. I noticed that he seemed really cold and distant as he hurried around the room getting dressed, finally looking for his shoes.

'Is anything wrong?' I asked him quietly.

'No, I'm just late. I've got to catch a flight in a few hours. You can order what you want from room service and then let yourself out,' he replied. At that point he was dressed and after he'd glanced at himself in the mirror by the door he left the room and I heard the door shut behind him.

I got out of bed and walked into the adjoining room, where I noticed a huge wad of £50 notes lying on the ornate coffee table. He's left too much money behind, I thought to myself as I eyed up what I thought was cab money. I then started to panic, but I realised that I didn't have his phone number so I found my mobile in my handbag and called Jasmine.

'That's your fee, sweetheart, but you need to give me 20 per cent,' she said bluntly.

My heart sank and I dropped the phone. It didn't make sense. I really liked Hamid and so I was mortified that he thought I was a prostitute. My mouth went dry and my whole body shook because I knew straight away that I'd just been paid for sex. Then everything else fell into place and I felt stupid for not seeing it, but how was I to know when I knew nothing about this game?

I'd got my hopes up and thought Hamid liked me but it wasn't like that at all because I'd been used. The way Jasmine had told me what to wear, the fact that Hamid hadn't called to arrange the date himself... now it all made sense. She was a madam and he was her client. He thinks I'm a hooker, I thought to myself in shock. I was mortified because I'd prepared myself for the date and had been so excited about it, but in the end it wasn't a date at all. I clasped the money in my hand and then my thoughts changed. I need this money, I decided. It's too bad, he's used me and Jasmine has too – it's just too bad, I told myself, trying to make myself feel better. I was angry with Jasmine because she'd trapped me and I'd most probably never speak to Hamid again, but the first thing I needed to do was to get out of the hotel – and fast. I got dressed, took the money and literally ran back to The Wellington. I opened the penthouse door and walked slowly into the bedroom. I'd hoped Natalie wasn't there because I needed to be alone. I undressed in the bathroom and climbed into the bath. As the hot water cascaded into the tub, I sat there and sobbed. I didn't know what to do or think, but for now I had some money and just wanted to scrub myself clean.

Over the next few days I was stewing and felt confused. I hid the money under my bed in a shoebox and tried to get on with my days, but I knew Jasmine would get in touch and I didn't know what to do. A few days later I called her myself and she told me that she wanted to talk over lunch.

I'd met escorts at parties before, but I'd never really understood about high-class prostitution until that day in the café in Knightsbridge. Jasmine was a madam and she explained her business to me: 'I've been escorting for years, Cassie, and have several girls working for me. I am very wealthy from it.' She then went on to tell me that she had five properties in London and a child to support. 'My child is in a private school and doesn't know what I do for a living. I had no life before now. I had a poor upbringing, but I love sex and money so I make the most of it.

'Cassie, you wouldn't have gone through with the date if I'd told you that Hamid had booked you: he's married. If I'd told you, you wouldn't have spent the night with him and had so much fun. You had a great night and you made some money at the same time. That money is peanuts to someone like Hamid so just spend it. I'm sorry it turned out like this, but I really thought you'd be happy when you got the money,' she said, her words tumbling out. When she finished, she looked at me, waiting for an answer.

The Madam

She'd made it all sound so simple but I still felt angry, used and confused. On the one hand, I was so angry because I'd been duped; I also felt used by a man and by Jasmine, too, and that hurt. I was also very confused because despite my anger and upset I'd still taken the money. I knew I had £5,000 stashed in my shoebox at the penthouse and, when I thought how much I actually needed that cash, the idea of spending it became appealing. I remembered the expensively dressed women at The Wellington and what Stacey had told me months ago about subsidising my modelling in other ways.

'Hamid liked you and he wanted to spend the night with you. Think of the money as him paying for you to get home. That amount of money wasn't anything to Hamid, anyway,' Jasmine said that day over lunch, as I sat there, dwelling on my confusion. 'Enjoy your money, Cassie, and try not to feel so hung up about it. It's the way this industry works, you know, and many girls like you don't have a choice. Many models do this, so don't worry.'

Because she'd made it clear about other models and Hamid's financial situation, I started to feel better about having taken it. I was only fooling myself, though: had I been in a better frame of mind then, I know I would have acted differently during this period.

When I left Jasmine at the café that day I don't think I'd really come to terms with what had happened. The whole experience was hard for me to deal with because, although I was no saint, I was not especially sexually advanced; I hadn't had that many sexual partners and I'd never even had a one-night stand. Now I know that I definitely couldn't find peace with myself: I was so wrapped up in a world where money really mattered that I eventually blotted out my thoughts and feelings about Jasmine and Hamid. I thought about all the friends I had, and how their lives seemed more luxurious than mine, and so that day I decided that I needed to try to put the night behind me and move on.

I walked down Sloane Street and gazed in the expensive shop windows. I then thought of the £5,000 waiting at home for me. I stood outside Chanel and looked at the shoes in the glitzy shop window. I then called Natalie and told her where the money was hidden, and we hit the shops together. We splashed out on clothes and jewellery, and that night I also partied hard. I had a fantastic time and buried my thoughts and feelings deep inside as I threw myself into partying. I wanted to forget that night with Hamid with a vengeance and that's exactly what I did.

All I was clear about was that I would never escort again. I knew 100 per cent that it just wasn't me. I still felt that I didn't know the difference between pure sex and making love and tended to get emotionally involved whenever I slept with someone. I only enjoy sex when I have feelings for that person unlike these girls who just love sex and it means nothing to them, I told myself. Soon after that, I realised that all Jasmine's 'friends' were also prostitutes. I hadn't come across escorting in such a blatant way before, but here it was, right under my nose.

What attracts young models to this trade is the glamour attached to it. The men have so much money that the girls suddenly get a taste of the amazing lifestyles of the men who use them. When they are in the company of these rich men, the models falsely think they're living the rich life, but in reality they're not. Escorting distorts everything because it provides the girls with a fix of the highlife, but it also gives them a completely false sense of security. They forget that they're only there with a rich man for a few hours at a time and they are just being used; that, if they get sucked in, eventually they will be thrown on the scrap heap with nothing to show for it.

In fact, a week later, Jasmine explained more about what she did as we sat together in the bar at The Wellington. 'I've worked with other celebrities and models just like you, Cassie. You should open your eyes a bit more. You'd be surprised who has done escort work: I've worked with tons of glamour girls. Every name has a price, Cassie, and when you're a name you can command up to £20,000 a night. Most of the glamour girls you know have escorted at some point in their career because as a model it's way too difficult to make ends meet at the start. Escorting is easy and financially lucrative, and it allows models to go out and party on the money they make.

'I do it loosely so no one questions me – I take girls to parties or I go to hotels. It's all so simple and no one questions anyone. Don't ever sit at a hotel bar on your own, Cassie, because it's a signal that you are a call girl,' she continued.

That night Jasmine asked me to think again about joining her on the game: in her mind she'd left it open. 'I know where you are out most nights, Cassie, so the offer is always there for you. Everybody has a price...' she repeated, tossed her raven hair over her shoulders and disappeared into the ladies'. I looked around the club and I wondered how many of the girls in there that night worked as escorts. However many or few it was, I certainly wasn't about to join in.

After that I'd often see Jasmine in clubs surrounded by footballers and other Page 3 girls, but I rarely sat at her table when I saw them all there, chatting to her. A month later I did go over and join her because I wanted to see how she was. That night, a Frenchman in her group took a shine to me. This man wasn't as extravagant as Hamid had been and he didn't beat about the bush. He was older, but attractive with dark hair and blue eyes and, although I was attracted to him, something within me was pulling me back. When I knew Jasmine was trying to strike up a deal, I suddenly felt angry with her for considering me one of her girls that night.

'Cassie is a difficult one,' Jasmine told the swarthy Frenchman, his dark, desperate blue eyes undressing me slowly, as we shared champagne together at the VIP table. 'She won't oblige, I'm afraid. Why don't you have a think about the new blonde model for tonight? I've just found her,' she continued quickly.

Jasmine was right: unfortunately, I'd had my first taste of escorting and, although the money was fantastic, I decided there and then that I wasn't going back for more. I felt terrible about what I'd done and spending the cash, but at that point in my life I was making bad decisions because I'd really lost my way.

The next day she called again and left a message. 'The Frenchman really wants you, Cassie. He's offering £4,000 to meet at the Grosvenor Hotel and then you can take it from there,' she explained, as I listened.

Even though I was still hard up and wasn't in a great

frame of mind, I knew that I could never escort again because it made me feel used and dirty. If I slept with a man, I wanted there to be feelings between us and I wasn't the type to give myself so easily to someone for any amount of money. I thought about that new blonde model. I knew exactly what she would have to go through that night if she met the Frenchman and how her first taste of escorting would eventually crush her; it was so easy to be reeled in.

The week after spending the night with Hamid, I really hit rock bottom. I think I'd reached the end of the road by becoming unknowingly part of something that had so disturbed and sickened me. I was taking drugs, I'd escorted and I was very much off balance by this point. I tried to bury those negative thoughts and feelings about myself, but they just kept coming back. The worst thing was that I'd lost sight of my career, but because I didn't know who to trust I didn't know who to turn to for help. I was constantly in touch with my family but obviously could not confide in them about the kind of life I was living. My poor mum didn't understand the kind of world I was inhabiting but she knew that something was not right. She constantly worried about me and I really hate that I caused her so much anxiety.

Slowly, but surely, the world I'd been living in was starting to sicken me. I hated its falseness, the letdowns and lies. I hated the drugs, the hookers, the unsavoury way girls made their money, how the men treated women... I hated the way this world got the better of girls, as it had done me, and I desperately wanted out.

Luckily for me, a new man came into my life and saved me.

Chapter Ten

Salvation

THE DAY AFTER I MET CELESTINE BABAYARO I FELT LIKE I'D STARTED MY LIFE OVER. It was the winter of 2003 and I remember lying exhausted underneath the black satin sheets in his bed and smiling. I was alone, but for the first time in months being alone actually felt good. Of course I was tired from the lack of sleep after the previous night, but I remember that my mind was crystal clear and I felt unusually happy; also refreshed and clean.

This clarity of mind and peace within me felt alien, but that morning I knew I'd changed my life. I normally feel suicidal and low after a big night out, I thought to myself; I normally fall apart if I wake up alone. That morning I knew that I had only a few hours of this precious time before Celestine got back from football training, so I had to get my thoughts together quickly. There were a lot of thoughts to get through and plenty of decisions to be made.

Until then I'd been in party mode so I never thought, What am I doing with my life? I was making bad decisions and focusing on the wrong things. My life as a glamour model had been spiralling out of control and I'd completely lost my way; drugs often clouded my mind so I was unable to make good decisions for myself. Because I was always tired, too, I wasn't motivated to work. Plus the party lifestyle was affecting my looks, which didn't help – I was pale and thin, my eyes had lost their sparkle and my skin was in really bad shape. Lack of work and money depressed me so I ended up partying more and that culminated in my not thinking straight through experiences like the escort episode. At first I'd wanted to mix with this crowd but the only thing that mattered to them was drugs and money, and I just didn't want to be with them any more. I didn't want to belong in that world any longer or to discover the key to it. Most of all, I wanted to find 'me' again and to start my life over.

What dawned on me most that morning, though, was that it was me who had made those choices: I'd chosen to model, I'd chosen to party and take drugs and I'd chosen to mix with superficial and dishonest people like Jasmine. I'd thought all this was making me into a stronger person and I was having fun, but it turned out to be far from those two things, with none of it filling the void within me. I fully understood that the scene was highly addictive and that it was tough as a young newcomer to say 'no', and that, rather than helping you down the right path, model agents don't guide you properly. But I was old enough and wiser – there wasn't any excuse now. I needed to take responsibility for my actions and get myself back on track; to fill the void with decent things, like working hard and spending time with people who really cared. I realised it wasn't too late for this and that if I learned from my mistakes and started to accept them then I could turn my life around. I knew and understood the world I'd been in, and I knew there was no excuse.

The main thing that helped me refocus was that I hadn't taken drugs the night before. I hadn't even wanted to, and that had helped me to think, understand and want to change. But the feeling of awareness wasn't just about waking up feeling clean; it was also about meeting Celestine. This man had shown me something different: that love, honesty and decent, hard-working people still existed out there and could help me. He made me feel like I was in fact a real person with real feelings and that 'me' was a nice, loving person, a person he wanted to spend time with. It felt like Celestine was a knight in shining armour, who had rescued me from a battleground where I'd been battered by my own poor choices and judgement. I'd been led astray by decadent, dishonest people and by taking drugs. Of course, I myself had made those choices but I know it would have helped if someone had guided me better, like Celestine did. I always tell people that being with Celestine Babayaro was like being in rehab and it's true because he changed my life and gave it new meaning.

I remember Tintin telling me about Celestine before I'd even spoken to him. We'd been introduced one night in a club and he'd apparently taken a shine to me. 'He's really gorgeous, Cassie, and he wants me to set up a date with you,' she'd said, as we sat in the living room together, watching TV.

'Yes, but I can't remember him at all,' I replied, disinterestedly. And that was true because, although Celestine had apparently been in the club a few times and we had chatted, I couldn't for the life of me picture his face. 'Also, I really don't know what I want right now, Tintin. I feel confused and down all the time. I don't think I can go through with dating someone right now, especially a footballer,' I explained and then I stopped the conversation and sat deep in thought.

At this point everything was getting me down: the people I was partying with, the partying itself, the drugs and the lack of modelling work. What's more, the recent situation with Jasmine had been the final straw. Things weren't going well for me at all. I couldn't rationalise or make decisions for myself because I was always so tired or on a comedown. The last thing I wanted was a man in my life and definitely not a flamboyant footballer.

'OK, well, let's see what happens,' she said, hugging me. 'Don't worry, Cassie, it will all come together for you.'

Thankfully, Tintin knew exactly what I needed, that I had to get away from the crowd in which I was mixing and be with someone different. She also knew Celestine was a decent guy and so she secretly instigated a night out.

One Friday Tintin told me we were going out. 'It's the end of the week and I need a night out, away from here,' she said.

She always worked so hard and, when I looked at her pale face, I knew I couldn't say no to her. 'Fine, I'll get dressed and let's go somewhere special,' I replied.

At that point, I hadn't been out for a few weeks because I hadn't felt like it, but I owed it to Tintin because she always looked out for me. I quickly dressed in a vest top and a pair of jeans and, before I knew it, who should appear to pick us up but Celestine!

'I'm Celestine,' he said, holding out his hand. 'I am so pleased to see you again.'

I looked over at Tintin and she smiled. 'You're terrible, Tintin!' I laughed.

Apparently, he'd asked Tintin for an introduction to me and he took us both out that night. We headed over to Browns in the West End. Once there, we ordered a bottle of champagne and sat down at a table in the corner to chat.

Celestine sat down next to me and we started to talk and I noticed how his eyes sparkled and what amazing skin he had. To be honest, at the start I could take it or leave it. He seemed charming enough and I was attracted to him, but I wasn't looking for a boyfriend and I wasn't in the right frame of mind to want to get involved with anyone. But because he had an aura about him and was a complete gentleman, I started to warm to the idea of seeing him again. Celestine wasn't over the top even though he had money, plus he wasn't flamboyant like the other players I'd met on the scene. Those positive points stuck in my mind when we left the club together and were standing outside on the pavement. 'Why don't you come back to mine, Cassie?' he asked politely, as we stood waiting for cabs. 'I have really enjoyed spending time with you tonight and I'd love to show you my home and talk more.'

'OK,' I replied, and soon we were sitting in a cab together on the way to his place in Kensington. I felt a comfort and warmth with Celestine and, looking back, I realise that was exactly what I was really craving inside.

Celestine's house was gorgeous, but not over the top. It was comfortable and clean. A gorgeously sweet, musky smell hit me when I walked through the door.

'Do you want a drink of anything?' he asked. I didn't feel like any more alcohol, so when I shook my head, he made some tea and we sat together on the sofa in the sumptuous living room. 'I can get you a tracksuit if you're cold, Cassie,' Celestine said, touching my arm. He could see that I had curled myself up in the corner of the sofa, but before I could answer he wandered off and returned with a huge Chelsea tracksuit. I felt comforted and warm as I snuggled up next to him and soon fell asleep. He then put me to bed and it felt so comforting just having him next to me.

'You can stay here as long as you want to, Cassie,' said the voice next to me.

I opened my eyes and looked up to see Celestine standing next to the bed, smiling. He looked like he was going off to play football, so I suddenly panicked that I'd overslept and thought I'd better leave. 'Oh, um, where are you going? I must go…' I muttered.

'I'm off to training, but, as soon as I get back, we can have lunch together. You seem really tired, Cassie, so just stay here and rest. I'd love you to stay,' he said, kissing my forehead and then he left the room.

I felt great comfort that morning as I dozed happily in his bed and when he returned and ran me a massive bubble bath I felt like a new, re-energised woman. We both spent the day relaxing and watching movies. Like I said earlier, I felt so different that day – secure and loved for the first time in years. We didn't have sex and it felt nice just being with him. The nicest feeling for me was that Celestine was caring. All he wanted was for me to be all right and to spend time with me. He told me his house was mine and that I could have anything I needed, even cuddles! When you are doing a lot of drugs and you party, you don't have cuddles and you don't have time. Celestine loved the warmth of cuddling me and the time he took stroking my head meant a lot to me.

I spent the next night there and again the next morning Celestine woke me up and went off to football training. 'You can stay or go, whatever you like, Cassie,' he said. 'If you do go, there's a cab fare on the table for you and I'll see you later on tonight perhaps...' And he wandered out the door.

I got up and found my mobile phone. I had forgotten to switch it on and suddenly panicked that I hadn't called home. 'I'm fine, Tintin,' I said to her on the phone. 'Tell Nat I'll be back in a few hours.' I hadn't been home for two days and I did worry about Natalie being alone.

'That's great, Cassie,' she said. 'When you get back you can tell me all about it!'

I showered, put on the tracksuit Celestine had given me and went into the living room. There, I spotted the money he had left on the side for my cab, but I didn't take it. I remembered the incident with Hamid and confidently left the house and waited in the road for a cab.

'Where did you get that top?' laughed the cab driver.

'Oh, a friend gave it to me,' I said, and I laughed to myself because I didn't care what the cab driver thought. I was on cloud nine. Suddenly I remembered the Walk of Shame when I would leave a hotel suite after a full night's partying. I felt relieved that I didn't have the same feelings that day as I headed home; also that that part of my life was now a closed chapter and I had finally found the strength to change. I felt relief because I had at last found someone who really cared.

Unfortunately, my feelings of happiness that day were marred slightly because of Natalie. She seemed upset when I opened the penthouse door. 'Where have you been?' she asked.

'With Celestine – I was having such a wonderful time, Nat, that I totally forgot everything. I've got so much to tell you!' I replied.

I couldn't wait to tell her about Celestine and also about the new and important decisions I'd made about my life; I couldn't wait to talk those decisions through with her and get her support. Perhaps Natalie and I could start this new journey together, I thought, but it wasn't as simple as that.

'I can't believe you just left me here like this, Cassie. You're so selfish! I thought we had an understanding,' she cried.

I couldn't believe what I was hearing. Here was my best friend, and it seemed to me in my euphoric state of mind that she was angry with me for having a nice time. I know I'd been out for two days and hadn't called her, but I had been so low a few nights before and I had needed time out. 'Nat, please understand,' I said calmly. 'Listen, I'm sorry I forgot to call, but I had to get away for a bit. I found someone really special and I feel like things are going to change. I feel like I can make a new start now.' I reached out and tried to hug her, but she just pulled away from me and stormed off into the bathroom.

146

Salvation

The difficulty was that Natalie and I depended on one another. I realised, as I stood speechless in our bedroom, that she must have felt lonely and left out and perhaps she didn't feel safe in the flat on her own. There were always different people there, either Tintin's or Jake's friends, or ours, but, because we were normally there together, we usually felt safe. Suddenly I felt terrible for leaving her like that and so I went and knocked on the bathroom door. 'I'm so sorry, Nat. Can we talk about it? Open the door and let's talk, like we always do,' I said quietly. But she ignored me and refused to open the door.

Initially I had wanted to pour all my thoughts out to her – thoughts about how I had finally met someone I liked, someone who wasn't into drugs and didn't just want sex… I wanted to tell her how I hadn't wanted to be 'out of it' with him, to explain to her how I had felt, Wow, I like this! I'm missing out and this is nice. She knew what I'd been through recently and it was such a big turning point for me. As I stood in front of the closed bathroom door, I realised that it was Natalie who was the one being selfish.

Natalie and I did, in fact, talk that day and we made some decisions. But, although we managed to make up in the end, she seemed to be warning me not to take Celestine too seriously. 'I agree that we need to get out of here, Cassie,' she said, after I'd finally told her that I wanted my life to change. 'Let's try to find somewhere else to live; it will be like a brand-new start. We can focus on what we actually moved to London for, and not the partying.'

She had listened to me and agreed that she felt the same. We both wanted to work and to take responsibility for our lives again. The flat was getting to us because there were too many people in there doing drugs at night. Sometimes we would be asleep and wake up to find some random man sitting at the bottom of our bed. The penthouse room had served its purpose but it was damaging us and we both agreed that our time at The Wellington was over.

Despite our new decision and understanding, Natalie still couldn't accept that there was a second person in my life. A few days later, I told her that I was off out again with Celestine. 'Nat, I'll see you tomorrow afternoon but call me if you need anything. Tintin is in tonight, so don't worry,' I said, kissing her. I'd chosen that night because Tintin would be in all evening, but Natalie just sat in the living room in silence. I knew when she didn't respond that when I got back the next day there would be another row. I did feel bad for Natalie, but I needed to enjoy my new love and so I left.

Of course the next day when I came back home we argued again. 'I can't take any more of this, Natalie. I'm leaving!' I shouted, after yet another slanging match. I went into the bathroom, showered, put on some clean clothes and left. I didn't know where I was going, so I wandered into the park nearby. My mobile rang.

'Where are you, sweetheart?' It was Celestine.

'I'm in the park. I had another argument with Natalie and I've left. Will you come and get me?' I asked.

Within minutes he was waiting in his car near The Wellington and he took me back to his house. He cuddled me a lot that day as I talked everything through with him. It was lovely, just having the warmth and support from someone I trusted.

That night we went for dinner together and, as we

Russell and I in happier times, before our relationship got out of hand.

© *Express Syndication*

Above: Marbella magic – my short break to Spain with James Hewitt was fun while it lasted.

Below: With Michael – I was heartbroken when we split.

© Matri

After I'd been with Michael for a while, I decided that a WAG's life was not enough for me and got my modelling career back on track.

Jeff Walker/www.epicpictures.co.uk

Above: The launch of *WAGs Boutique* – the girls from Better Half (*from left to right*) Charlotte Mears, Jadene Bircham, Heather Swan, Elle Isaac and me.

Below: They think it's all over … the final show of the series.

© *Rex Features*

Above: Goaaaal! Charlotte and I prove that we can play the game as well as watch it.
We celebrated our win with some well-earned fizzy stuff.

© *Rex Features*

Below: With the celebrity soccer six.

Charlotte and I, glammed up for a night out. We stayed good friends after *WAGs Boutique* had finished.

Above: This was the first time I'd seen Papa since I was 18. Now that I'm older, I can accept the kind of relationship we have and I know he's there if I need him.

Below: With my lovely mum. I don't know where I would be without her and the rest of my brilliant family.

Above: At a Cartier polo event. (*From left to right*) Ruth, Martine, Nicky, Tru, Gemma and Beth.

Below: With my gorgeous boyfriend, Lee, with whom I have finally found love and security.

shared a pizza, Celestine took time to help me focus. 'You need to get your independence back, Cassie,' he said. 'It's the only way you're ever going to make it. You need to stand on your own two feet. You've relied on Natalie for too long now and look where it's got you! You're a model in your own right and it's not about her any more. You need to refocus alone and work harder. It'll pay off, believe me.'

And he was right: it was time to move on. So, on top of all the other decisions I had made that week, Natalie was just another one.

That night we also made love. It was just as I imagined: warm, caring and intimate. The next morning Celestine took me back to The Wellington so that I could get more clothes. I didn't know if Nat would be in, but she was. 'He's just another typical footballer, Cassie. You need to be careful,' she said. 'It won't last. Make sure you're not away from here too long, otherwise I'll be gone when you get back.'

But after what Celestine had said the night before, I didn't need her any more. This time I was following my heart and, until I was proved wrong, he was the one I wanted to be with.

Celestine introduced me to the whole world of footballers and it was a shock to my system. I thought I'd experienced the London scene with all its trappings, but this was a different ballgame. I noticed at once that footballers have the celebrity status that girls want and straight away I knew I couldn't handle it. The first night when we met at Browns it didn't bother me because I didn't have feelings for him, but, as we started to go out in the West End, our evenings together became increasingly strained because of the female attention he received.

It happened on one of our first dates together. 'Move up, love,' said the busty blonde girl, who stood in front of our table. We were sitting together in Browns and several girls had come up and were dancing provocatively near our table. They appeared from nowhere but their intentions were very clear.

'I'm with Celestine,' I said to the girl, who then licked her lips and flounced off. She knew full well that we were together, but she didn't seem to care. 'Why are they doing this?' I asked him, almost in tears.

'Just ignore it, Cassie. I've only got eyes for you and they know it,' he said, putting his arm around me.

I felt better, but when it happened again that night I just didn't know what to do. 'Hi, Celestine, I'm a big fan,' said a brunette, who'd approached our table within minutes of the other girl.

I stood up and walked to the ladies'. I wanted to leave, but I pulled myself together in the toilet and then headed back to the table. By this time, the brunette had rudely sat in my seat and was busy whispering in Celestine's ear. She looked up and smiled knowingly at me. I felt so stupid, standing there alone. 'I think I should go, Celestine,' I said, and started to walk to the exit.

'Cassie, Cassie…' I heard his voice behind me. 'Listen, let's go home and get some sleep. You're tired,' he said lovingly.

'What was she saying to you?' I asked him angrily.

'She didn't say anything, sweetheart. She's just a party girl I've known for years. You need to try to trust me.'

And with that we left the club in silence and went back to his. I just couldn't find it in me to trust him, probably because of what I'd gone through with Papa.

After that night, I couldn't stop thinking about the girl and, as the days and weeks went by, I knew I was finding the relationship way too hard. We would hang out at places like Prive, 57 Jermyn Street and The Wellington, and most nights Celestine and I had great fun. But the female attention got to me in the end and I found myself being jealous and aggressive with him, and it must have got on his nerves. Although he never complained about it, in the end I couldn't take it any more and just backed off.

'What's wrong, Cassie?' he asked me on the phone one night. It was late and because I'd heard a rumour about Celestine and another woman I had left Prive early that evening.

'I can't talk right now, Celestine. I'm tired. I'll ring you tomorrow,' I said, and hung up as my eyes welled up with tears. I never called him back, and the next day, even though he called and called, I couldn't muster up the strength to talk to him. I didn't know what to believe about the rumour, but I knew I didn't have it in me to see the relationship through. I just didn't want to get hurt, so I never gave Celestine a chance to show me otherwise.

In hindsight, it wasn't necessarily the right decision.

'Don't take the calls, Cassie,' Natalie had said. 'He's seeing someone else.'

The words hurt like hell and, because I didn't know what to believe, her words made me stick with my decision to cut Celestine out of my life. I didn't want to talk to him about it and I didn't want to have to make a decision; I just wanted it all to blow over and feel secure. Looking back, how I wish I'd given Celestine another chance.

Even though at the time I thought I was getting myself back together, I was still a weak and vulnerable person when it came to men. Now that I've grown up and I'm stronger, I probably could handle it, but back then it was just another problem I didn't want to deal with. I hadn't dealt with Papa and I couldn't take pain like that again at that point. There were too many other things that I needed to work on for myself and having men problems just didn't fit in. I feel sad when I remember that time: I know in my heart that Celestine and I could have been something more, but, because of my own shortcomings, I never let it be.

After that, I once saw Celestine out. 'You're lovely, Cassie,' he said. 'I'll never forget you.'

The warmth I felt with him resurfaced and I was sad as I walked away, but what he said meant a lot – and it still does.

Natalie and I got on with our lives following this and, although I was hurt because I'd lost someone special, I was determined to keep my newfound strength, free from drugs, too much partying and the wayward people I had in my life. I wanted to follow a better path and take control for myself. Regardless of which men came in and out of my life, I was just determined to rediscover 'me'.

Chapter Eleven

Prince Charming

I NEVER DREAMED THAT I'D BE LINKED TO A MEMBER OF THE ROYAL FAMILY, BUT THEN, DESPITE ITS DRAWBACKS, THAT'S THE BEAUTY OF THE LONDON PARTY SCENE. With all its sleaze, drugs and superficiality, a random encounter with a unique person is always a possibility and that's what made the scene so alluring to me.

Meeting Prince Harry was random and he was also unique. But what I realised was that, despite our incredibly different lifestyles and vocations, we had one thing in common: we both enjoyed the unknown and that night Harry and I experienced that feeling together. Unlike me, he wasn't a regular in Chinawhite. I also wasn't the type to mix with royalty, but, as we sat and chatted happily together, there was such an ease between us that it almost felt surreal.

Mentally, I was in a very happy place when Harry and I

met in the spring of 2004. I was 21, and Natalie and I had just got out of The Wellington penthouse. We didn't leave there on bad terms, we just felt that it was time to move on and, in fact, I still go there to this day. Work was coming in again and, because I'd put a lid on the escorting episode and felt relief at having ditched the drugs, I really felt like 'me' was coming back for good.

After a brief stint at Mum's, we found ourselves a new place in the heart of Belgravia. Strictly speaking, we couldn't really afford to live in such an exclusive area and always struggled to pay our rent there. In fact, we ended up in quite a lot of debt trying to cover our costs. However, the flat was gorgeous and had stunning views. It was nicely decorated in creams and browns, and felt like home straight away. There was a beautiful freestanding bath and a black marble shower room. We loved our new home, just as we loved our comeback on the modelling scene. Work was picking up again and, because I wasn't taking any drugs, I felt motivated and it was paying off. I was booked on all the usual magazine shoots again and started travelling to Europe regularly to shoot various lingerie campaigns; I was also doing *Playboy* and *Italian Vogue*. For the first time in a year I had proper money coming in and so I was really starting to sort myself out. Then, to our joy, Natalie and I also shot our first TV show: *Poor Little Rich Girls*.

The show was a life-swap reality show where one person with a privileged, plush lifestyle would swap places with someone who was less well-off. They would then show how well or badly each girl coped living the other's life. Natalie and I were the 'rich girls' and, while one of us would stay at home in the flat, the other would take the 'poor' girl around London. The concept was fun and, even though it was a gruelling few weeks filming the show, we loved every minute of it. The exposure was fantastic and, because we were hard at work, I had toned down the partying. Although I was still in touch with Stacey and we occasionally went out together, she wasn't at the forefront of my life as she had been at one time. Natalie and I were also getting on better and, despite the blip with Celestine, I was generally feeling much happier all round.

The night that I met Prince Harry I'd been enjoying drinks out with Stacey and a mutual friend called Mischa that we'd met on the circuit.

'Who is all the security for?' I remember asking Mischa as we sat at the VIP bar.

'I have no idea,' she replied nonchalantly, as she sat eyeing up a tall blond man, who'd been staring at her legs ever since we entered the club.

That particular night Stacey had joined us for drinks after I'd been working at a promotional event in Earl's Court. Because we were all tired we'd just wanted to catch up and then head home to bed. I felt exhausted after being on my feet all day, talking to punters at the car show, and all I wanted to do was to sit down, enjoy my drink at the bar and get back.

Suddenly a massive entourage of young men came in and sat down in the corner. There must have been at least twenty of them, most of them dressed in khakis and polo shirts. A few stragglers were in dark formal suits and those few were ushering the others around. They were in high spirits when they were shown to their tables and soon began ordering drinks. The men looked younger than the usual Chinawhite party crowd and they were also dressed differently. 'They stand out a mile!' I said to Mischa, as we carefully eyed up the group.

'I wonder who they are,' she said, but we just couldn't place them.

When Stacey came back from the ladies' we noticed one of the men from the group heading over towards us. We sat bolt upright because we all felt something exciting was going to happen. At this point, I smoothed down my skirt, took my lip-gloss from my handbag and carefully glossed my lips. I knew I wasn't dressed properly that night because I hadn't gone home to change after work, but I still looked good in my denim mini skirt and fitted black shirt.

'Will you three beautiful ladies come and join us for cocktails and champagne?' asked the burly man in the black suit. 'I'm looking after the men over there and they have asked me to call you over to join them. They have a lot of drinks to share around and no one to share them with.'

Stacey, Mischa and I grinned, then happily followed the man to one of the tables. I felt slightly giddy so I sat down at the table. There were so many men standing around us and I noticed that several of them were already unsteady from drinking. I helped myself to a glass of water and looked for Mischa and Stacey. Already they were busy chatting to two blond youngsters in the group. 'Are you OK, Cassie?' Mischa shouted, noticing I wasn't with them.

'I'll be fine!' I shouted over to her. 'I just need ten minutes sitting down. My feet are killing me!' I drank the water and decided to help myself to a glass of champagne.

I remember clearly the events that unfolded next. 'Let

me help you,' said the young man who had sat down next to me. 'Do you want more water or would you just like the champagne?' he asked kindly.

'Champagne would be fine,' I replied, smiling. I didn't even look at his face at that point, but accepted the glass. 'I was feeling a bit faint, but I feel better now that I've had the water,' I told him.

'Yes, I bet you were – it's very hot in here and there are a lot of drunken people milling about!' he said.

I laughed inside because he spoke with such a plummy accent. It was lovely, though, and he seemed very sweet-natured.

'Do you come here often? I know it's a tacky question, but I just wondered,' he asked politely.

'Oh, yes, all the time. Do you?' I asked.

'No, this is the first time. I'm enjoying seeing something different and having a fun night out with my friends. I fancied a change from where we normally go out. I quite like it in here!' he said and grinned.

I then turned to ask him where he normally went partying, but I suddenly realised who he was. Before I could get my words out, Harry had asked me my name and what I did. My nerves started to get the better of me so I decided to turn the tables on him. 'What about you, what's your name?' I smiled, chipping in. I knew exactly who he was, but suddenly I was fascinated.

'I'm Harry,' he said.

I laughed inside because, when he told me he was Harry, he just carried on chatting as if he was an ordinary person. He was so charming and natural, and that made him all the more endearing. Of course I found him handsome, but it wasn't something I was thinking about because I was just bowled over because I was sitting and chatting normally to Prince Harry! When Harry left, I felt really glad I had met someone so special, but who also seemed so nice.

'Goodbye, Cassie! It was a pleasure to meet you,' Harry said warmly and shook my hand.

'Bye, Harry – come back to Chinawhite soon!' I said, smiling, and then Harry left.

I walked over to where Mischa and Stacey were standing and told them what had happened. 'I chatted with Prince Harry!' I said animatedly.

'Yes, we saw that! He seemed to like you, Cassie,' they laughed.

I smiled, but I knew that, although Harry was single and gorgeous, we had just had a nice, pleasant conversation. 'Oh, don't be silly, Mischa – he would never want to date a glamour girl! We shared a fun and unusual moment together and that's enough for me,' I said.

At this, the three of us left the club together and I went back home. Thoughts of Harry were far from my mind that night as I lay in bed because I had a big photo shoot to get through the next morning.

The next day, a Thursday, I woke up, thinking my alarm was going off but it was my mobile. 'Cassie, were you with Harry last night?' asked a fraught journalist from the *Sun*. I knew her from the party circuit and, because she was always so nice, I had agreed to swap numbers with her ages ago in case I needed any help with press in the future. I hadn't really worked with the press before but, for some reason, I felt I could trust her. That morning she wasn't the same: she was rushed and aggressive. 'What did he say? Did you kiss? Why were you together?' The questions were probing and harsh.

In the end, I couldn't handle the call and there didn't seem any point or relevance to the questions, so I told her I had to go and hung up, shaking. What do I do? I asked myself. Actually, I had no idea what to do.

The phone rang again and I answered it. This time, it was a journalist from the *People*, offering me £2,000 to talk about Prince Harry. 'I don't have anything to talk about,' I told him clearly. This was madness – I didn't have anything to say that was worth £2,000!

After that, I switched the phone off and headed into the bathroom: I needed to prepare for my photo shoot and I just wanted to concentrate on that. I took off my dressing gown and then realised I could hear Natalie shouting on her mobile in the living room. 'Was she really? No, I wasn't there. I'll ask her. I can't believe she's done that!' she was saying loudly.

I stood there in silence, wondering what she was talking about and to whom. Then I heard Natalie knock on the bathroom door and she came in. 'Cassie, what's going on?' she asked curtly. 'I have had calls from my agent about you and Prince Harry. Why didn't you tell me about this? Are you going to do an interview?'

'About *what*? There's nothing to talk about,' I said quickly. 'This has all been blown out of proportion, Natalie, and I don't understand why it's annoyed you.'

But all she told me was that I should take a shower and that we needed to chat in the living room.

An hour later, Natalie sat me down on the sofa and

explained that, because the press knew we were friends, they were hassling her agent to get to me. She seemed annoyed about that, but at this point she was helpful and explained that, if I did an interview with the tabloids, I would get a good amount of publicity and some decent money. All I needed to do was a phone interview and they would put the cheque in the post. I trusted her and, because I was angry with the journalist from the *Sun*, I quickly called back the reporter at the *People*.

'We can do your phone interview in an hour, Cassie. You need to give us as much detail as possible so that we can pay you the £2,000,' he explained.

'But nothing happened,' I replied.

'OK – well, have a think about all the details from the moment you met him to the moment he left. We need to know everything he said,' he advised and then hung up.

An hour later, I was telling the journalist about the evening before. 'We just chatted and he left. He is good-looking and polite. He asked me what my name was and what I did for a living,' I said quickly on the phone. At this point, I still couldn't understand what the story would be because there wasn't anything to it! I couldn't understand why those questions would command £2,000, but then the journalist told me I had given him enough.

'Make sure you switch your phone off and please don't talk to anyone else about this until Sunday,' he said aggressively. 'You'll lose your money if this story appears anywhere else.'

So I did as he asked. I went to my shoot and looked forward to seeing the paper on Sunday and treating myself to some new clothes!

In fact, I didn't know at that time that a front-page story in a Sunday tabloid can command thousands of pounds, plus I never signed a contract or asked to approve the copy and I would instinctively know that I had to do that now. That Saturday afternoon all I wanted to do was to go out and celebrate my first-ever real press interview. 'We can get the papers on the way home from the club, Stacey!' I laughed down the phone.

'Yes, Cas, let's go and celebrate, and then read your interview together on the way back in the cab,' she said.

That night I remember feeling so excited as we hit the dance floor at Aura. I was out with a few of my closest friends and they kept saying how they were all so proud of me for getting myself into the papers. I bought everyone champagne and, when I left the club at closing time, I was feeling very happy. I remember running as fast as I could to the newsstand on the corner of Regent Street.

The newspaper man was busy stacking up bundles of papers when I spotted the front page of *The People*. It said in not so many words that I'd canoodled with Prince Harry! My whole body shook when I read the headline. 'I didn't say that!'

'Say what, love?' he asked, looking at me in a very bemused way.

'That I canoodled with Prince Harry!'

Stacey caught up with me and tried to calm me down. She held my arm. 'Come on, Cassie, let's go,' she said knowingly, hailing a cab for us. 'Let's go home.'

Together in the back of the cab, we sat huddled over the paper. As I read each word carefully, I realised that the interview I had given had been completely distorted. The reporter had asked me if Harry was flirting with me, but when I opened the paper the headline said something completely different. The story actually ran that I was with Prince Harry all night, and that we were canoodling. It was such a lie! I had given the correct and truthful information to the *People*, but this was all twisted. The piece said Prince Harry was all over me, but he was just chatting. I had just sat with this nice young man and spoken to him over a few drinks.

When I got back to the flat, I just climbed straight into bed and tried to sleep. At least it doesn't say anything nasty about me, I thought. I can learn from this, I told myself. I then fell asleep and was just thankful that I hadn't been made out to be something I wasn't. This was my first taste of the world of the tabloid media and, although they hadn't hurt me, they had got the better of me but I was determined not to let the same thing happen again.

But, as if that wasn't enough, things were about to get worse. I woke on that fateful Sunday and heard Natalie shouting from the hallway in the flat. 'There's a journalist banging on our door, threatening me. They're saying, if I don't let them in, they'll tell everyone that you're an escort!' she screamed.

I remember my whole body freezing. 'Escort?' I said to myself quietly. I was so drained with tiredness from the events of the night before that I couldn't even be bothered to get up from the bed. I'm not an escort, I thought to myself, sick with fear. As I thought harder, I felt panic and a surge of helplessness come over me. 'Wait a minute, I need to get my head together,' I said, quietly remembering the Jasmine episode at The Wellington. 'I need to eat something and then let's try to work out what to do.'

But it was too late: Natalie had walked out of the bedroom and slammed the door. What if they have proof and pictures? What if they know Jasmine? My mind was racing and I felt so scared. As I lay there, motionless in bed, I was afraid, but what made things worse was Natalie and how she seemed to completely dis me after that morning.

That day, Natalie appeared unable to help me. At the time, she knew the press a lot better than I did because, as I said before, she had already had dealings with them herself. Naturally, I turned to her for help when the press were threatening us both outside our front door. I got up and tried to ignore the buzzing sound, resonating from the intercom throughout the flat. I put on my dressing gown and went into the living room.

'I can't speak to you, Cassie,' Natalie sobbed. 'We can't be friends any more. I can't help you with this terrible situation you've got yourself into, so please go away!'

I couldn't believe what I was hearing; I went back into my bedroom, sat on my bed and cried. I have never felt so alone and I was completely distraught. Thoughts of Papa crept into my mind and so I cried even more.

After a while, I knew I had to try to pull myself together. I showered and dressed, then took the intercom off the hook and switched my mobile off. I felt trapped in the flat. The only person I called that day was Stacey. At least she would be there for me, I thought, feeling better. And she was – she stood by me in my hour of need and turned out to be a true friend, one of the few true friends I have ever made in my life. 'You aren't with an agency, Cas, so don't worry, sweetheart. You're not an escort, so it's not a problem – they're just trying to blackmail you,' she reassured me. 'They can't write something like that when it's not true. To be safe, just ignore them, don't speak to anyone or answer your phone. Try to carry on as normal. I'll pick you up tonight and let's go out.'

I felt better after Stacey calmed me down, but it's like they always say, the past does come back to haunt you and that Sunday night it certainly did. I had unwittingly acted like an escort that one time and, although I hadn't chosen to do it, more than ever I now regretted that I'd taken the money Hamid left for me and I'd spent it.

That Sunday night, I went to Pangaea nightclub with Stacey and Tim to try to forget about the day. At the time, I felt confident that nothing bad could be written about me because I wasn't with an agency or escorting, and I decided to do what Stacey suggested: to try to get on with my weekend. That evening at the club there was a special night on and I knew it might help me forget the day's events. When we got there, I was still worried and was very tearful. Because I felt scared, I just kept drinking to forget about the interview I'd done the few days beforehand.

But, as we left, things deteriorated further. Outside, the paparazzi were waiting for me like dogs. 'Cassie, over here!', 'Look at me, Cassie!', 'Smile, Cassie!'… The pavement was awash with cameras and flashbulbs. I assumed they were there because of the story in the *People* that day. I knew it was normal that they would want to snap someone if they had been in the papers that day; it was also normal for them to be waiting there on a Sunday night whenever Pangaea held an event. But suddenly a crumpled newspaper was thrust in my face. I remember staring in disbelief at the front page and then going straight into meltdown. I couldn't deal with it and I collapsed in shock on the pavement.

I felt limp when Stacey pulled me to my feet and into a waiting cab. I couldn't hear her voice when she told me she was taking me back to her flat. 'You need to try to get some sleep, Cassie,' she said warmly, as she undid my shoes and took my dress off. She tucked me up in the bed and sat with me until I felt strong enough to speak.

'Will you stay with me, Stacey?' I asked weakly. 'I don't know what to do now – I feel like everyone thinks I am bad. I don't know what to do!'

But Stacey simply stroked my head and told me to try to sleep. 'I'll stay with you here tonight in the room and let's work through this together tomorrow,' she suggested.

All I wanted to do was curl up in a ball and die. The front page of the *Sun* had brought all the guilt back and also reminded me of the one time that I had encountered the world of escorting. But the main thing was that I didn't want to bring shame on my family. That night I tried to sleep, but my head was crammed with negative thoughts and questions. This just wasn't fair! Why are they doing this to me? I asked myself over and over. I hadn't hurt them; I was never publicity seeking, but, for some reason, they had just turned on me.

The next morning, Stacey woke me with a cup of tea. 'I have to go to a shoot today but I'll be back later to talk. I left it as long as I could before waking you because I thought you needed to sleep in,' she said.

When she left, I got out of bed and locked myself in the room. By now, I was so disturbed that I didn't want to face Stacey when she came home. I spent the whole day in bed, thinking and worrying. When she returned, I still couldn't face anyone and so I stayed put in bed. 'Come out, Cassie. Are you OK?' I could hear her saying, as she knocked softly on the door. 'I'll leave your dinner outside. You need to eat, sweetheart.' With that, she wandered off.

But I couldn't unlock the door because I couldn't face her or the rest of the world. I felt helpless because the way the *Sun* had written the piece was so clever and everyone would believe what they said, or so it seemed to me. I also felt helpless not being able to do anything about it because I didn't know exactly what they knew. I realised that I had to sit and swallow it, and that hurt. For two days I lay and watched the door. Stacey came and went, leaving plates of food outside the door and then collecting them before she went to bed. I could hear her sigh as she picked up yet another plate of uneaten toast.

On the third morning I woke to hear my brother Ben's voice at the door. 'Can I come in, Cassie? It's me, Ben. It's just you and me now, Cassie,' he asked softly.

I remembered the bond that he and I had shared during our times together after Papa had left us and I remembered what Mum had told me when I had kissed Ben on the plane at Gatwick Airport all those years ago. I had to let him in that morning. I realised I wanted Ben to be the one to help me, just as I had protected him from being hurt emotionally over Papa, all those years ago.

Ben had driven straight from Kent to Stacey's flat because my family knew that at this point I was suicidal.

Prince Charming

Stacey had to call him because she wanted to make sure that I had all the support I could get – she knew my family would be the ones to make a difference. If Stacey had left me alone and not called Ben, I know I would have done something silly.

After a while I got up and unlocked the door.

'Hey, Cassie, it's me!'

I saw Ben's face smiling at me. I was relieved to see him and fell into his arms. 'Thanks for coming, Ben. I don't know what to do. Is Mum OK? I'm so ashamed of what it said in the paper, Ben. People believe the press and what will Mum think?' The words tumbled out but I felt so weak that I couldn't concentrate on what I was saying or how.

'Mum says not to worry and that she loves you regardless, Cassie. Mum wouldn't believe it anyway. She said it's not true so she doesn't care,' he said, hugging me. 'We all want you to feel safe and loved right now so don't worry about anything. We are all proud of you. I am here for you, Cassie, like you've always been for me.'

Ben stayed that day, and we talked things through and decided that we all needed to try to forget what had happened. I eventually got my strength back and I managed to move on, but of course this all took time. If it hadn't been for Stacey and my family, I don't know if I would still be alive. Also, the story died. I wasn't that well known anyway, so it faded away but the *Sun* have never been positive about me since. I don't think I've ever really recovered from what was written about me and it still hurts if I ever hear people referring to that article. After that, the days became a blur but somehow I did get over it and I pulled myself through with the help of my family,

Stacey and some kind of inner strength that I managed to muster from somewhere. You can either lie here and suffer, or just get on, I told myself over and over again. I really wanted to get on.

In the end I stayed at Stacey's for a few weeks and, although I pulled myself together over the Harry incident, there was still the issue with Natalie. She only called once to see how I was, but then I felt it was only out of guilt and I knew, at the end of the day, that she was no longer my friend. In fact, the very last time that I saw her was on the Sunday when the story broke. When I went back to get the rest of my things from Belgravia, I made sure that Natalie was out. I moved my stuff out and then got the phone call that I expected from her as she asked where I was. As it turned out, she was also concerned about the rent!

'I don't care if you can't afford the rent, Natalie,' I told her harshly. 'You let me down and you said you wanted to cut all ties with me. So that's what I've done: I have cut all ties!' I hung up and blocked all thoughts of Natalie from my mind. My life had been in ruins and she hadn't given a damn, so now neither would I.

A month or so later, I found out that Natalie left the Belgravia flat without paying the rent. Eventually, we both received Court Summons but Mum settled my debt.

After that, Natalie became quite well known on the celebrity scene. She went on to date Simon from Blue and made her name that way. I still have her number and we do speak, but we will never be friends again. If I see her out, I will never spend large amounts of time with her. She knows she's a closed chapter in my life now.

After that difficult period I stayed with Stacey because I

needed to get myself back together mentally. Despite the Harry story, I still wanted to do well as a model and so I started to focus hard again. Stacey was great and got me more promotional work, and I shot for many more magazines like *Fast Car* and *Italian Vogue*. I also signed up with two other big model agencies, Supermodel Agency and Sugar Babes, because I wanted to get more work.

Mentally, I don't know how I picked myself up after my run-in with the press – it really was the worst thing I'd ever experienced. I still don't really know how I didn't just give up; so many times in my life I have felt like throwing in the towel. I've made mistakes but I guess that's all part of growing up. Other people have skeletons in their closet but it's not easy for me to forget about mine – I'm constantly reminded of them and, even today, people say things to me about being an escort and it really hurts.

Somehow, I did manage to get myself back together, though – perhaps I'm stronger than I give myself credit for. I thought to myself, It's done now, so get on with it! I'd had bad luck, but life's generally unfair. I haven't had it easy, but I think people have it much harder than me. I was dealt those cards and that was the way my life was mapped out. Yes, my father left me, I was bullied and my friends let me down, but I definitely chose this life and industry and those friends. And, yes, I didn't know how tough it would be at the beginning and what path I would follow, but I carried on learning the pitfalls day by day. I knew I'd come a long way and it had been hard, but I also knew that, if I battled through it all, I could make it work. Today people say to my boyfriend Lee, 'Wasn't she a brass [prostitute]?' That's so hard, but Lee and I just ignore it.

If something bad happens to me now, I say to myself, What doesn't kill me will only make me stronger. I know my brush with the escort world and coming off drugs has done that. Really, my run-in with the media also only made me stronger. I think what Natalie, Papa and the bullies did weakened me considerably, but over time I managed to cope very well with it all. And, as I started to make better decisions for myself, so my strength resurfaced again and I became bolder and more independent than ever before.

Chapter Twelve

Brand New Man

WHEN RUSSELL BRAND TOLD ME HE LOVED ME, I COULDN'T QUITE BELIEVE IT. We'd been dating on and off for a year and it'd been working well between us as a casual fling. Both of us seemed to prefer it that way. Then one day he just came out with it. 'I want to be with you, Cassie. Let's be together like a proper couple. I love you,' he suddenly blurted out during a romantic dinner in a quaint Hampstead restaurant.

At first, I was speechless because I'd never thought of Russell as boyfriend material, but, after a few months, we became a proper, committed couple.

It was in the autumn of 2004 that we'd first met while I was having lunch with friends in a pub in Hampstead. 'You're gorgeous,' he told me after he'd approached me by the bar.

I remember thinking, This man is different, but eccentric –

I haven't ever met a man like this. His dark eyes and swarthy looks also reminded me of Johnny Depp! But it was his natural openness that struck me most of all. From the start of our love affair, Russell was always honest about the person he was inside, plus, if he didn't like something or someone, he'd be blunt about it. For me, those qualities were particularly refreshing because up until then I'd been surrounded by a superficial world, where people didn't speak their minds for fear of looking stupid or uncool. Russell also showed me something different in life and that was how to be happy and confident with the person you were. 'Don't be afraid to be yourself, Cassie,' he'd say. 'You're gorgeous throughout and people see that.'

On our first date we went to a warm-up comedy gig in a pub in North London. I had never gone on a date like that before, but Russell picked me up and, although I had my reservations about him, I ended up having a really fantastic and interesting night.

'I was a drug addict and was hooked on crack and heroin,' he confessed in the pub that night. 'I'm also addicted to sex.'

As I sipped a glass of wine while Russell stuck to water, I listened in silence. There was a lot to digest from that first date, but I felt for him and understood where he was coming from. The only thing was that, because of the things he told me, I accepted early on that he wouldn't be great boyfriend material. I was still 21 at the time and had my own insecurities and issues that I was working through. Adding Russell's into the mix would be too much for me to handle, I thought.

Brand New Man

After that first date, I would normally go and support him at one of his comedy nights or we would hang out together at Russell's flat in Hampstead or meet for dinner. Then, when we eventually became lovers, that set-up also worked for a long time. If I didn't have anything to do, I would ring Russell up and we'd go out for dinner. I fancied him and he fancied me, and, because we also got on really well, it seemed perfect and I felt in control, which was nice.

We'd been seeing each other like this for a few months when Russell suddenly sat me down and said warmly that he wanted us to be more committed. He told me that he would love to have a proper one-on-one relationship with me and that I was the one he wanted to be with. Like I said, I was shocked, but after a while I was actually really happy about it, so I decided to try. We never argue and things are good between us, I thought to myself afterwards. We have a laugh together and I enjoy fooling around with him at his flat. Sometimes we act like a couple of kids together. I was sitting in my bedroom at Stacey's when I decided that I would give our relationship a shot. 'I'm going to commit to him. I do care about him, even if he is quite erratic sometimes,' I decided. The next evening I told Russell that I wanted to make things work with him and be his girlfriend.

As well as feeling in control of things between us, what was also amazing during this time was how Russell really encouraged me to enjoy myself doing the simple things in life. To be fair, I'd got into partying again after splitting from Celestine but it wasn't to the same extent as I had done before. I still enjoyed going out, but, as with

Celestine, Russell showed me how we could have as good a time at home. 'Why do you need to go out all the time, Cassie?' he'd often ask me when I'd be getting ready to go to a media event or celebrity party with one of my friends. 'Why don't you stay in with me? We should do more things together as a couple.'

The next night I would remember what he'd said and do just that. I actually started to enjoy myself more and more with Russell at his flat – I loved it, in fact. I loved those warm, cosy evenings in front of the TV with him or when we'd mess around with his cat, Morrissey.

On the other hand, I knew the parties were paying off. I was gaining more press and also featuring more in magazines. Russell didn't stop me going out, he just opened my eyes to yet another way of living and helped me find a balance. Sometimes, if I'd decided to go out on my own, I'd crave being at Russell's afterwards.

On one particular occasion when I'd been drinking all night, Russell pushed me further into his arms. 'Can I come back and see you?' I asked, slurring my words down the phone. 'I miss you and want to be near you.' It must have been about 6am, but he was happy that I wanted to see him.

'Come here, sweetheart. I'll be waiting up for you when you come,' he said lovingly. When I finally arrived at his flat, although I was in a drunken state, he was so kind and patient with me. 'Don't worry, Cassie,' he said, as he ran me a bath. 'You can always come here and be with me. I'd love it if you started thinking about me a bit more, though. I wanted to be with you this evening, but you wanted to go out with your friends and now look at you!'

And he was right: earlier that day, he'd asked me over for dinner, but I'd said no. As I sat in the hot bubble bath, Russell leaned over the tub and hugged me. I felt safe. By the time we finished talking about what he wanted and needed from me, it was almost dawn. He gave me fruit and water, and because I wasn't tired he took me to the cinema.

After that night, Russell and I genuinely started to get emotionally attached to one another and I felt really happy. I'd committed myself to him and had decided to start being there for him whenever he needed me. I also decided to cut back more on going out.

But, after that conversation and my decision to commit, our relationship sadly started to crack. Those cracks appeared when I tried to involve him in 'my' life. 'Why don't you come with me tonight, Russell? It will be good for your profile to be seen at this party,' I'd tell him. Not only did I want him to meet my friends and to spend time out with him, but I also thought he would understand the importance of work-related functions.

Sometimes he would come with me, but after a while he started to behave somewhat erratically when we were out at functions together. It seemed to me as if he didn't like the fact that the paparazzi wanted to take photos of me. 'Why are they taking pictures of you, Cassie? I thought I was the famous one!' he would say, if we were coming out of a club together and the paparazzi were there. At the time I just ignored these remarks but, when it really started to get me down, I ended up going out alone.

That year, Russell and I decided to go away together to America for Christmas. I was excited at the prospect of spending two weeks in the States with him and really didn't know what to expect. Although I had slight doubts because of the idiosyncratic behaviour I had just started to witness, I thought a break away would do us some good. 'It'll be so nice for us, Cassie,' he'd said, when he suddenly asked me to go away. 'I want to see the sights of America with you, Cassie. It'll be the trip of a lifetime!'

He spent hours trawling the Internet, planning the journey, and I agreed that it would be a nice break for us because we would be together, away from work and away from the London scene for a few weeks.

We decided to fly to LA and then drive south to San Francisco and see the sights along the way. I was so excited when we landed at LAX and, despite being tired and jetlagged, I couldn't wait to collect our hire car and start the holiday. Unfortunately, it was then that things started to fall apart and my excitement began to turn to despair.

The first thing that we fell out about was when Russell asked me to stop smoking. 'Please, Cassie,' he complained at the airport when I lit a cigarette outside. 'It's driving me mad! It's such a disgusting habit and it's ruining your health, and mine.'

I agreed with what he said, so after we'd collected the car I bought several boxes of Nicotine patches. I really wanted to stop smoking for Russell because I knew how annoying it would be for him to share a car and spend time with a smoker. After we set off, I wore the patches rigorously.

Unfortunately, as the journey progressed, the patches took away my appetite. I was already finding it hard giving up smoking, but not eating on top of that was making me tired. 'You've got an awful eating disorder, Cassie,' Russell said, as he sat in the passenger seat. 'You've got serious problems,' he would continue. But I knew I didn't have an eating disorder and it created problems between us. As a model I do have to watch my weight, but I was – and always have been – a healthy eater. At that point I just didn't feel like eating with the patches on. Russell knew that I hated Chinese and Indian food, but kept saying that we should eat them. I couldn't believe how ridiculous he was being, but I soon realised during the early days of the trip that he was very insistent about certain things.

'Put my CD back on, Cassie!' I remember him saying from the passenger seat. Russell wanted to listen to his music on the CD player in the car so I would kindly put on his Beach Boys CD and drive as he sat happily listening to it. Whenever he fell asleep I would change the CD because the music was grating on me, but then he would suddenly wake up and ask for the CD to be changed back. The worst thing was that I did all the driving for us because Russell can't drive. I would end up behind the wheel for at least six hours a day, listening to terrible music!

At the start it was nice in the car because of the scenery and because we were both happy to be in the States and were relaxed. In the end, the arguments over the food or my patches and then the music he played completely dominated and spoiled the trip.

The day before Christmas Day Russell told me he'd never been given a Christmas gift. 'I'd love something special this year, Cassie,' he said, but, because the trip had cost me an arm and a leg, I really didn't want to spend much more money. 'I want an iPod,' he told me that morning.

So, as I sat behind the wheel on the way to San Francisco, I decided that when we arrived I'd take Russell

Christmas shopping. I felt bad that he had never had a nice Christmas present and thought perhaps getting him an iPod might improve things between us.

When we were in the shop, he happened to choose the most expensive iPod, even though he knew I probably couldn't really afford it. In the end, I bought him what he wanted. When we got back to the car, I was really fed up, but somehow I let it go. Funnily enough, Russell bought me exactly what he wanted that day. I got a pair of white D&G sunglasses that I didn't even want!

When the ten days came to an end, I felt completely drained. I couldn't wait to get back home to the UK, but unfortunately the tension between Russell and me didn't ease when we landed at Heathrow on New Year's Eve. We'd agreed to head to my parents' because they were throwing a party for us. 'I can't wait to see Mum and Patrick!' I told Russell, as the plane hit the runway. It had been so long and I knew seeing them might break the ice between us. At Heathrow we were both really tired. My parents had driven to collect us, so I felt happy knowing that I wouldn't have to do any more travelling that day.

But it turned out that Russell had changed his mind. 'I don't want to come with you,' he suddenly piped up, as we got through Customs.

My jaw dropped, but he stood there, clutching his suitcase and looking upset. By that point, I felt so frustrated with him. 'Go back to London, Russell! I'll see you in a week or so!' I snapped and started to walk off. But he was soon following close behind me.

While on holiday, Russell would have to attend Narcotics Anonymous meetings wherever we were, but I understood what he was going through and we would talk about it at length. I would take him to meetings wherever we were because he didn't want to fall off the wagon. During the ten days that we were away, he would ring up the organisation to find out where he could go to a meeting in the town we were heading to. He went three times in all, but it was fine because I knew he had to attend those meetings for the rest of his life and it was important to him, so I was happy to do it. He needed that support in his life and he was determined not to fail again.

Anyway, we met Mum and Patrick, and travelled home to their house in Kent for the party. I had a fantastic night, but at 12.30, Russell announced that he was going home. 'Are you coming or not?' he asked, looking forlorn.

By then I was so fed up that I told him to do whatever he wanted. He left me at the party and went to bed. The next morning I woke up and he'd gone! As I looked at the empty side of the bed, I felt relief. All I wanted was to be left alone and I didn't want to see or call him for a few weeks. I decided to stay at Mum's and then, when I felt ready to head back to London, I called him and we agreed to meet up.

Amazingly, we did manage to patch things up and Russell did say sorry and so I forgave him. I also wanted to give him a second chance. At that point I had to move out of the flat where I was living in Maida Vale. I'd started to look in North London so Russell and I could see each other easily, but then I decided that I really wanted to live South of the river near my friends, plus North London is much more expensive. At first, Russell agreed to help me flat-hunt and suggested I stay with him until I found somewhere.

Over the next few weeks, things were fine between us but, one afternoon, as we clambered into a black cab to look at a few places I'd seen advertised, Russell suddenly decided that he didn't want to come with me.

'We need to head to Chelsea,' I told the cab driver.

'Stop, stop the cab! I'm not going anywhere near Chelsea with you!' Russell suddenly proclaimed at the top of his voice. He then opened the cab door and ran off up Hampstead High Street.

I sat and watched all this unfold in front of me. But I knew it was pointless to ask him what was wrong and so I just closed the cab door and left him to it. He was upset that day, but that was Russell. One day he would be happy and cuddly, the next snappy and moody. Over time it became clear that Russell was too much for me to handle.

One other bizarre display also sticks in my mind. Russell loved his cat Morrissey and always gave him specific cat food. If he was busy filming, I would take care of Morrissey for him. One day, because I was on a shoot, I didn't have enough time to get the right food and so I rushed home with a tin of kitekat. Like a king, Morrissey ate it, but I stupidly left the tin on the sideboard. When Russell came home he completely lost it. As soon as he saw the empty tin on the sideboard, he started shouting at me, 'This poor defenceless cat can't get food for himself, Cassie! What have you done? What were you thinking of, giving him the wrong food?'

I couldn't believe that a grown man of 28 was scolding me about cat food, but that was Russell all over.

Russell isn't Russell Brand the TV star. Like so many other celebrities, that's an act he puts on – and he does it very well at that. In real life he has mood swings and seems very contradictory. Over time, the honest and open, caring person I had first met just wasn't the same any more. The more time I spent with him, the more I grew to realise that he is an anxious man. By Christmas 2004, I knew it was over.

We finally split up the day after my 22nd birthday. It was the start of 2005 and I wanted everything to begin perfectly. I desperately wanted Russell to join my friends and me at a dinner and club night, but I understood that he couldn't make it when he said he was away filming. My big day came and Russell called, saying he was coming back, but he was way too tired to come out. I was gutted when he told me on the phone that he wasn't coming because I really wanted to have a special night with him.

'Happy Birthday, love,' he said, when he finally came home that evening.

'Thanks,' I replied. But I didn't get a kiss or a hug, and he hadn't even bought me a card! He then stood in the hallway, making excuse after excuse about the party, so in the end I got dressed and left alone.

I had a fantastic night with my friends at Aura and, because I felt neglected by him, I was determined not to go home to him. It was dawn when I finally put my key in the door of his flat.

Russell was already up. 'Nice time?' he asked, under his breath.

'Yes, thanks,' I replied curtly and headed into the bathroom.

An hour later as I lay in the bath, I heard the front door shut. I got out of the bath and walked into the living room. It smelled strange. I wandered into the bedroom and opened the drawer by the bed. Russell and I kept condoms there and I always knew what type and how many. The bedroom smells funny, I thought to myself. 'There's only one condom left!' I said, under my breath. I shut the drawer and went into the kitchen. There was a wine glass in the sink and the bottle of wine that I had opened for myself before I went out was completely empty.

Russell hadn't even bothered to conceal what he'd done! I rang him straight away and he admitted that he had had a woman in the flat that night and said sorry. 'I am rubbish at all this, Cassie,' he said, in tears.

But I didn't care about his tears, and so I hung up and, without a second thought, I packed my things and left his flat. I didn't want to give him another chance after that. Russell did call again that day and he told me he didn't want me to go, but he didn't have the right to treat me like that.

I must have been prepared, though, because I got over Russell really quickly. Maybe I was just more resilient to letdowns and pain by then and wouldn't let it get to me. I'd spent almost a year with him and, yes, it hurt that he cheated on me, but the hurt went. After all, I'd been through so much and letting a man get in the way just wasn't going to happen. I remembered that the guy had issues and probably always will, plus he wasn't good enough for me. Saying that, I never loved Russell or was in love with him – I reckon I wouldn't let myself. The way he sometimes spoke to me was pretty bad and I felt strong enough in myself to move on and forget about him. I was thankful to him, though, for showing me how to get a better balance in my life, plus I felt happy with myself, and so I happily took that positivity with me into my next phase.

Chapter Thirteen

Starting Over

AFTER SPLITTING WITH RUSSELL I MOVED TO MY FRIEND JADE'S HOUSE IN WINDSOR. I wanted to get my thoughts together about where I wanted to be living next and how I wanted to move forward with my career. On the personal front, I knew I was over the worst and had two real focuses: to get to the top of the modelling ladder and to be living back in London, but alone. As far as my career was concerned, I also wanted to work harder, but now I knew that I wanted to look at different avenues.

It was January 2005 and I was doing quite well with my model bookings anyway. I was appearing in the usual lads' magazines like *FHM* and *Loaded*, and I'd also started to shoot abroad a lot more. I really enjoyed the times I'd spend away on business in luxurious places such as Monaco and Southern Spain. Photographers would cover all my expenses and send me on location shoots where I would shoot during the day on the beach or by the pool at the villas I stayed in. Those shoots were nice little earners and, although the hours were long, I always stayed in fantastic accommodation and was looked after impeccably.

During the time that I was homeless, I decided that I really wanted to take on a manager. Because I'd enjoyed filming *Poor Little Rich Girls*, I knew TV was where I needed to be, but, for that to happen again, I knew that I would need some sort of management behind me. I felt lucky when I signed a year's exclusive contract with a friend of mine called Craig Pass. Chatty and smart, he was on the party scene and so he knew everyone. He also knew everything about me – my qualities and strengths and the weaknesses that he now told me he wanted to work on. 'I see real potential in you, Cassie. I think you have something special,' he told me one night when we were out enjoying drinks at Embassy nightclub.

I listened to what he had to say and realised that, for the first time in my life, here was someone who was determined to draw out and build on my true potential as a model. We both knew I was a natural in front of the camera but that I also had a real knack of getting people's attention. 'It's not just about your looks, Cassie,' he explained. 'You're bubbly and confident, but you also make people smile. I've seen it so many times when we're out.'

It was fantastic sitting with Craig that night; I felt good about myself because I'd turned my life around and now it was paying off. I was obviously giving off a good feeling wherever I went, which in turn meant that I was becoming a stronger and happier woman by the day. But most of all I felt fantastic because now I was the real 'me'. 'When do we start?' I asked.

'Tomorrow. Come round to my office and let's sign a contract,' he replied happily.

Up until that point, as I said, I had never had management before, but it made such a difference when I signed up with Unleashed Publicity. Instead of relying on my agent getting phone calls about castings and shoots, the next morning Craig explained how he would strategise for me, approach the magazines and pitch me in a particular way. 'You have a good CV and a great portfolio!' he exclaimed. 'Leave it with me and I'll direct you in the right way. We are also going to sort out a few media events for you so you start reconnecting with the press and the celebrity world. I'll call you in a few days when I get the invitations arranged. I'll always escort you, so don't worry,' he added.

After that first meeting when Craig sat down and went through the ropes with me, it all made perfect sense. I was tired of having no real direction and I was disappointed with the way I had been left to my own devices as a young and naive model; I had never been taught how to work the system or how I could really progress. Until now, it felt as if I'd been at everyone else's mercy and unable to give my own input and ideas. Signing up with Craig was such an exciting progression for me and I welcomed it with open arms.

Funnily enough, I also met another glamour model around the same time – I won't use her real name, I'll call her Sally. At this time, Stacey had moved to Dubai because she'd met a man out there while on holiday in January 2004. I was missing her company and, because Natalie and I hadn't really cemented our friendship again since the Harry saga, Sally came into my life at a great time. Sally was very successful simply because she possessed a raw and unique energy. Unlike me, she really didn't need to be pushed or directed and like Natalie she knew what she wanted from the job and how to get it. When I met Sally, her drive and determination made me realise more than ever what I was lacking. 'You need to push yourself more, Cassie,' she'd said on our first photo shoot together. 'You must have ambition, otherwise you wouldn't be in this business, so you need to draw it out. Some models need others to do that for them and there's nothing wrong with that. It's all about confidence at the end of the day and you need to build yours up even more.'

She was spot-on. This girl is something else, I thought to myself. Small and slender, she was incredibly photogenic. I'd come into contact with so many models over the previous two years through work and partying, but I'd only gelled with a few and Sally was one of them.

'You also need to start networking again, Cassie,' she told me one evening as we ate dinner together.

'I know,' I told her. 'My new manager has said the same. But it all got too much for me before now and I want to adopt a different approach this time around. It didn't work before because I was so young and naive, and I got swept up in it all.'

I went on to tell Sally about everything: how I'd got in with the wrong crowd and how I wanted to live their life and belong; about how partying and drugs had taken over my life and how taking drugs had caused me to make too many mistakes. 'I'm lucky to still be in this game. I haven't given up yet,' I said finally.

Sally sat and listened intently. I knew her life as a model had had a different start. She'd stayed in her home town, where she lived because of her boyfriend. She was in love with him and he loved her, and she felt secure within herself. She also felt confident and had stayed sane.

'I don't think London is always the best place to start if you're alone, Cassie,' she remarked. 'It can ruin a young model if they don't have someone there for them to rely on when they come home at night. But don't be despondent about the past, Cassie, you're only 22 and still have an amazing future and career ahead of you. You need to find and develop that ambition you had at the start. You have succeeded this far on your own, so it's obvious you've still got it in you.'

That night, Sally struck a chord. I felt so happy that I'd met Craig and then Sally, who had equally inspired me and given me new hope. I had that ambition inside me and, although other things like the partying, the drugs and the superficial people I'd met had sent me on another path, the modelling ambition was still within me, ready and waiting to come out again in full force.

We agreed to meet up in London when Sally came down for work. I remembered her words and set my heart on pushing myself forward. I was also determined to look after myself better, mentally and physically. At that point, I hadn't taken drugs for a year, but it had taken that long to really get myself back to normal. That normality meant a Cassie who was strong-willed, fun-loving, independent, responsible and beautiful, and that's exactly the woman Craig had talked about when he first signed me up.

Mixing with the media and celebrities soon became an integral part of my job. It wasn't about partying and letting my hair down, it was purely networking. It was great because I was footloose and fancy-free, and that made me feel anything was possible out there. If I do get asked out by someone famous, then I have a choice to take them up on it or not, I would think to myself. I wasn't looking to date a celebrity, but I was open to that if it happened – just as any other young girl would be.

Most of the magazine parties I would go to were heaving with celebrities and industry types anyway, but, with my professional hat on, instead of letting loose and relaxing I would network hard. I was much more conscientious about attending restaurant and club launches, magazine parties and film premieres, where the paparazzi would snap me whenever I walked in. I'd go anywhere where the media were and where they might notice me. 'It's for the good of your career,' explained Craig each week. 'You're underachieving and you need to get out there!'

At the time, the London glamour scene consisted of high-profile models like Jordan and then the lesser-known Page 3 girls like Leilani and Michelle Marsh. I knew that I was coming back into the modelling world in a more professional way, but there I was finally, and looking back I was eternally grateful to Craig. He would always be there with me, introducing me to new people and making sure I was OK. 'You need to be in the papers as much as you can, Cassie,' he would say, and he was right.

Starting Over

If I was spotted with someone famous, my name would fly straight into the papers and, in turn, the magazines would want me more. It's the way the industry works now, and did a few years back, and I was lucky to have the looks and personality to work with that. 'If you want to make it as a model in the glamour world, sometimes you need to add more strings to your bow,' Craig would add. 'Girls do use their celebrity connections, but celebrities likewise use their status and profile to get together with prettier girls. You need to understand that there is no real career for a "glamour girl" any more. Not one that pays, anyway. It's not about doing glamour shoots any more, it's about how quickly you can become a name and a face. It's about the people you mix with, the people you date and the stories that might involve you. If you control that, then it's easy. It's the whole package, Cassie, and you have it at your fingertips – but only if you're sensible about it.'

Just as I took on Craig, I also wanted to get back to London and start over again. I really wanted my own place, my independence and space to breathe. For the first time in my life, as with my modelling, I didn't want to rely on a friend, boyfriend or my family. Apart from Mum, Ben and Stacey, everyone had let me down. Since starting out as a model, I had never experienced that sense of independence and I presumed that having that space would allow me to really focus on making progress alone in my career and also in myself. I needed to build up my strengths and, to do that, it was down to me and me alone, not Mum, Stacey, Natalie or Russell, but Cassie herself, and alone.

I had always been let down by people and was

disappointed that I'd trusted and loved people who did not deserve me. Saying that, I always believe you learn something from everyone you meet and, although these people had taught me a tough lesson, I felt stronger and ready for a new chapter. I knew that I had a good heart and was a good person, and that's what kept me going. There was still a lot in me, still a long journey ahead professionally, a lot of drive and determination to succeed and getting a new place alone was a starting point.

It was spring 2005 when I started to flat-hunt properly. By chance I found a rundown, two-bedroom flat in Hatton Garden, East London. Hatton Garden isn't the usual sort of area that a young career girl would look for somewhere to live, especially a model! But something was telling me to go for it and so I followed my gut instinct. I was making a new start in my life, so I thought that turning a scruffy council flat riddled with dirt and mice into a comfortable home would be cleansing and cathartic. After negotiating with the owner, I secured the flat for £1,000 a month. For a two-bedroom place in central London, it was a great deal, and because the owner didn't want a deposit I felt confident I could make it work financially. Of course, for me on my own it was a lot of money, with bills on top of the rent, but knowing that I would have to clear that amount every month with my modelling work meant that I needed to be really focused and work much, much harder. It was a worry at first, but I knew I could do it if I put all my energy into my modelling.

When I first viewed the flat, it looked terrible but I had no idea how bad it really was until I moved in one weekend when I realised it was more than filthy. The worst part was the kitchen. There was old, mouldy food smeared everywhere – on the walls, windowsills and floor. Mice were running around in the cabinets and mites climbing up the grey, stained curtains. It was really disgusting but somehow I knew I could make the place home.

I set to work scrubbing the flat from top to bottom: I covered the floors in bleach and detergent, bought new tiles for the kitchen, curtains for all the rooms, new TVs for my room and the living room, and bundles of white bed linen. I scrubbed the bathroom and painted every room in a fresh white. The furniture in the living room and bedrooms were usable, so I knew that cosmetically, if I cleaned it all up properly and bought all the trimmings, my new home would look great. During those first few days, I didn't care how long I worked cleaning because I wanted my home so much.

By Sunday night the place was finally finished. I had transformed it myself and was satisfied, happy and proud. On the Monday I set to work on my career. My home was clean and tidy, and work just needed to follow to pay the bills. I spent the morning speaking to Craig and making a few calls to my model agent. By the afternoon I was coasting because the magazines all booked me for shoots the following week and Craig was busy talking to the press and various TV companies for me, plus he had tickets to a few media parties that week.

By the end of the first month at Hatton Garden, I had regular money coming in and was able to pay all my bills and rent alone, and on time. Plus, I had enough to spend on going out, if I needed to. I was supporting myself alone and it felt great. I didn't need drink or drugs, and I didn't need a boyfriend either. I had found a new strength within myself; that was enough to make me happy. It felt like Cassie was invincible without anything or anyone propping her up.

Then one evening I got a call from Sally. 'Fancy a night out, Cassie? I'm coming down to London tomorrow,' she said.

'Definitely!' I replied. I hadn't been out for a few months now because of work and the flat, so I really needed a break and to let my hair down. When I wasn't working abroad or doing photo shoots in town, Sally and I would sometimes meet up for dinner, but I'd been so wrapped up in supporting myself in the flat and working that I hadn't had much fun for a while and felt I deserved it. I loved spending time with Sally because we always had a great laugh.

When we met up, Sally told me that she'd split up with her boyfriend and that she needed to leave where she was living to get over him. She then asked if she could move into my flat. At first, I was hesitant because I was doing so well alone. Whenever I came home tired after work or from being abroad, I loved my own space and I loved the feeling that I was finally supporting myself alone. I'd created this sanctuary and space for myself, and I was thriving on it. 'I really need time to think, Sal. Is that OK? Come down next weekend again and then I'll decide,' I said, knowing full well that, because I knew Sally needed me, I'd let her move in.

And so we gave it a shot. It's normal for me to like helping other girls out because close friends like Stacey and Craig had helped me. I knew what it felt like for Sally because I'd been through the same thing when I split with

192

Starting Over

Damian a few years earlier. If it hadn't been for Stacey, who knows where I might have ended up? I wanted to give something back to Sally. She was the one injecting the fun into my life again and she had given me some fantastic support and advice when we met, so I wanted to help her out. That's what friends are for, I thought to myself, while telling Sally that she could move in whenever she liked. We were enjoying drinks at The Sanderson Hotel and when she smiled broadly and hugged me tightly at the plush bar I really felt I'd made the right decision.

Of course, the advantage of all this was the benefit of splitting the rent, but I also enjoyed Sally's friendship and company. It wasn't a case of me relying on her or needing her around, it was pure enjoyment and fun with her. Plus, I knew that we would work well living together because we were both really tidy and would cook and clean together and she also understood my need for space. I was right because, as soon as Sally moved in, our living together worked really well. We both shared everything, such as buying and cooking food and all the household chores, and there was never any stress between us. Naturally, we grew closer and spent more time out networking together. From her partying and through her other model friends, Sally had got involved with the footballer party crowd. She loved the scene and its glamour and, because of my friendship with her, I started to step in and out of that world whenever I wanted. This time was actually the start of the whole WAGs and footballers craze and it was normal to see girls vying more than ever to be seen in the company of footballers.

After a few months, I was slowly becoming more a part

of that scene. At weekends, I started to enjoy having drinks with the Chelsea team players at Embassy and Chinawhite. They were all kind and friendly to me and I loved the fact that they knew how to have good fun. Although I wasn't as close to the footballer crowd as Sally was, I met players like John Terry and Joe Cole. Sally had introduced me to them and, when we went out, I would sometimes end up partying with them, nothing more and nothing less.

Chapter Fourteen

Marbella Magic

As well as partying with Sally's fun-loving footballer crowd, I was still busy keeping my head down and attending celebrity events and media parties in the West End. It was at one of these events during the summer of 2005 that I met James Hewitt.

When James first approached me at a glitzy magazine launch, I was struck by his charm, intelligence and wit. Although there wasn't a physical attraction between us, we clicked straight away because we were both focusing hard on our profiles. James had just filmed *Celebrity Wrestling* for ITV, so I knew that he was very well connected and obviously that he was famous. As we chatted over champagne and canapés at the bar in the Sanderson Hotel, he seemed genuinely interested in my career and so we spent time that night discussing each other's professional goals and ambitions.

For my part, I just enjoyed his company. He was fascinating and fun and, although at first I assumed he simply enjoyed having a pretty girl on his arm that night, he really seemed to warm to me like a friend. 'Let's meet again this week,' he said suddenly at the bash. 'I'd love to take you to see Elton John sing in Marbella! We'll have fun, Cassie, and we can network there. It's in a few days' time and we would have a fantastic three days. Please come. I've got a private jet booked already!'

It was a huge invitation and, of course, I was taken aback, but that was the beauty of James Hewitt. He was spontaneous and kind.

'Oh, James, I'm not sure,' I replied. I'd only been talking to him for an hour by that point, so it would have been way too much for me to hop on a private jet with a stranger and fly off into the sunset! Even though I was sure that we would travel to Marbella as friends and I felt comfortable with him, I didn't know him. 'Listen, I was hoping to leave this party early tonight because I have to work tomorrow. Would you mind if we chat about this tomorrow because I'm in a hurry to get home,' I explained.

'I understand. You need your beauty sleep,' he said, looking slightly forlorn. 'But please give me your mobile number before you head off into the night and let's discuss Marbella tomorrow. It'll be fun, Cassie – and no strings attached!'

I asked James for his mobile and quickly typed my number into it. We said our goodbyes, but, when I left the party, thoughts of the Marbella trip disappeared from my mind because I had a huge *Playboy* location shoot to do the next day.

Marbella Magic

It was 9am the next morning when James rang my mobile. 'How about flying on Wednesday then?' he blurted out.

I was flattered by his insistence, but the thought of flying anywhere with a stranger in two days' time still didn't appeal. 'Um, I'm not sure, James. Can we at least meet up for dinner first?' I asked, smiling to myself.

'I'll take you for dinner then. How about tonight?' he asked, and so, when I'd finished my photo shoot that evening, I caught a cab to Fulham to meet him.

That night, as we chatted over dinner at a cosy gastro-pub near James's flat, I found him even more fascinating than I'd done at the magazine bash. James came from a totally different world from mine: he had connections all over the world and was well read and clever. He talked about his experiences in the Army and all the countries he'd visited. But he didn't mention Diana and I didn't ask.

The nicest thing was that he was more than happy to discuss my little world for hours. Over dinner he boosted my confidence and, just as Craig and Sally had done, he made me feel I had so much more to achieve as a model. 'Look at you, Cassie,' he said, as we were finishing our dessert. 'You're beautiful, funny and clever. You should definitely think about doing more TV work. It will really challenge you and you seem to need that right now.'

I listened intently to all the sound advice he gave me that evening and I really felt inspired. When the bill arrived, I remember feeling totally rejuvenated by this man. 'I'd love to come with you tomorrow, James,' I told him, as we left the restaurant together.

After that meal, I knew I would have a fantastic three days, that I would experience a lot with James and that he would look after me well. I assumed that he wanted female company for a few days and that he had chosen me because he liked me. In fact, he seemed like a father figure to me and I felt safe.

'Great! I'm pleased you've come round to the idea. I'll collect you from Hatton Garden at 7am sharp. Bye for now!' he smiled, and flagged me down a cab.

The only thing bothering me by the time I got home was what to wear! I'd never been on a private jet before or with someone as sophisticated as James Hewitt. When I climbed into bed I couldn't sleep and so I ended up getting up at 5am to pack. I threw a few smart, but sexy, strapless dresses and a couple of plain bikinis into my suitcase and tried to relax. If I see something nice in Marbella, I'll just buy it when I'm there, I told myself and then fell asleep.

At 7am the doorbell went and it was James. Because it was very early, we didn't speak much as we drove to Farnborough Airport together, but I felt excited and glad that I'd decided to make the trip with him. Then things became very odd. 'Is that Max Clifford over there?' I asked James, as we got out of the car in front of the airport. I was sure that the famous publicist Max Clifford was standing waiting by the revolving doors with what must have been his wife. 'He's waving over at us!' I exclaimed. I waved back because I already knew Max: in the aftermath of the Prince Harry stories, I'd sought some advice from him. Although he had been pleasant and helpful, I'd always felt slightly intimidated.

'Yes, that's Max Clifford all right!' laughed James, as he handed our luggage over to one of the airport attendants. 'Max and his wife are joining us on the trip.'

Marbella Magic

Suddenly I felt really uneasy and questions started to flood my mind. The first problem was that I hadn't told James about the Prince Harry situation because it wasn't relevant, but now, because Max was there at the airport, it probably was. I wondered if he knew that I was coming on the trip with James. And did James know about Harry and me? Should I tell him? And what should I say to Max? Why hadn't James told me Max Clifford was coming with us? As we walked over to where he was waiting, I decided just to bear with it and hope that we wouldn't be spending the whole three days with him.

Then, from out of nowhere, the comedian Bobby Davro appeared with girlfriend! At that point, as I shook hands with Max and Bobby and kissed their partners, I suddenly felt uncomfortable. I was a 22-year-old model with all these 40-something couples! Actually, I felt a bit silly and completely out of my depth. Pull yourself together, Cassie, I told myself. Just enjoy the trip and then move on.

We clambered on to the small jet that was waiting on the runway. Obviously, it was way too late to cancel or pull out, but I still felt uneasy. 'I'm quite scared of flying, James,' I told him, as he showed me to my seat. 'Do you mind if I sit alone at the front of the jet?'

'Of course not, Cassie, you do as you wish,' he said.

As we flew to Marbella, I sat alone and tight-lipped at the front of the jet while the others sat at the back, laughing and chatting together. When we landed at the airport I was much calmer and more relaxed about the situation with Max. As soon as I felt the warm Spanish sun on my skin, I felt really glad that I'd made the trip with James despite the questions I still had in my mind. We were then chauffeur-driven en masse to a stunning five-star hotel in Puerto Banus. If you know Marbella well, then there's only one amazing hotel there, where only the richest of people will stay.

I knew James had really gone out of his way for me when we pulled up outside the Puente Romano Hotel and were ushered into the reception hall. The opulent hotel and its surroundings were out of this world! Lush, tropical gardens surrounded us and I could see a stretch of white-tinged golden sand on the hotel's private beach. As he and I stood at the reception area, I knew I didn't need to worry about the sleeping arrangements. We hadn't once shown any signs of wanting anything sexual with each other so it didn't surprise me when James asked if I would like my own room. Because he was being such a gentleman and we were friends, I told him I'd be fine if we had two single beds in the same room. Also, I really didn't want him to fork out for another room just for me because the trip must have already cost him an arm and a leg.

After we'd settled into our room, we went for dinner alone. It was nice and relaxed as we ate by candlelight, overlooking the exquisite floodlit hotel swimming pool. The summer air was sultry and close, and I sensed a feeling of excitement around me because many of the other hotel guests were talking about going into Puerto Banus for a night of cocktails and clubbing. I was feeling tired when we finished dinner, though, so I told James that I wanted to go to sleep. I wanted to feel refreshed for the next day and the Elton John concert. James had told me that he had got us VIP seats and planned an extravagant dinner afterwards, but I was hoping that Max and Bobby wouldn't be joining us.

Marbella Magic

The next morning we sunbathed by the pool and shopped in the quaint streets of Puerto Banus. I bought a new Roberto Cavalli bikini and some diamanté Dior sandals for the beach. It was all so glamorous as James and I wandered in and out of the designer boutiques dotted around the harbour area. We spotted Rod Stewart and his girlfriend Penny Lancaster having lunch near the harbour and several footballers that I knew, also busy shopping. That night I dressed in a pale-blue and yellow Versace dress with a plunging neckline. 'You look sensational, Cassie!' James gasped, as I twirled in front of the mirror. The yellow fabric set off my deep suntan really well and I was happy with the final result.

We then sped off in a chauffeur-driven car to the venue and found our VIP seats that were right next to the stage! When Elton finally appeared, the whole audience erupted. I smiled over at James, who handed me a glass of champagne and kissed my cheek. I had such a fantastic time with him in the VIP area as we laughed, danced and sang together. Max Clifford and his wife, and Bobby Davro and his girlfriend were standing right behind us, but by that point I didn't care because all I wanted to do was enjoy myself with James. The whole night was really memorable.

The next day was our last in Marbella. We spent the day relaxing by the pool at the hotel and then got ready for our final dinner. I was having such a pleasant time, but, after the excitement of the night before had finally died down, I started to wonder about Max again and if James knew about Harry and me. At dinner, James began by telling me about the mistakes he'd made in the aftermath of the death of Diana and how he still missed her.

I listened intently, thinking all the while about telling him about my encounter with Harry. 'Everyone makes mistakes, James,' I replied, trying to comfort him. 'It's part of life. I think, so long as we can learn from our mistakes and strive to be better people, then that makes all the difference. The people that are important in your life will always be able to forgive you anyway. What doesn't kill you can only make you stronger,' I said, remembering the tough times I'd experienced in my past and how my family had been my rock.

We continued chatting and I told him my story of how I had encountered Harry at the nightclub and the dreadful press that had unfolded afterwards. Probably because of how close he had been to Diana, James seemed keen to find out what I had thought of her son.

The next day we flew back to London and said our goodbyes outside my flat. James and I saw each other a couple of times after that, but the friendship just fizzled out. I really liked him because when I was with him I felt like a princess. He took me to some wonderful places and was a true gentleman. I can understand what Diana saw in him because he knows how to make a girl feel special! I didn't want anything from him romance-wise and also, at that point, I didn't need anything from a man either, which is why we worked well as friends – I was just happy to have his company.

Chapter Fifteen

Footloose

WHEN I SPOTTED HIM AT THE LAVISH MAGAZINE POKER PARTY, I RECOGNISED HIM STRAIGHT AWAY, BUT JEAN-CHRISTOPHE NOVELLI WAS EVEN BETTER LOOKING IN THE FLESH. Also, I could tell immediately that he was an expert with the girls. As he sat playing poker in the corner of the trendy nightclub, several women were busy swooning over him. Jean-Christophe oozed sex appeal and, just as he'd captured those women's hearts, he quickly captured mine, too.

It was late August 2005 when Craig escorted me to the party at Pascha nightclub. After he'd wandered off into the throng of revellers, I'd suddenly found myself networking alone. Pascha was heaving with leggy blonde models, the usual celebrities nibbling sushi and canapés, and hundreds of swanky media types dressed in smart black Prada suits, many of them busy watching the poker matches. But through the sea of glamour our eyes finally met as I stood alone at the bar. I kept laughing because whenever Jean-Christophe stopped playing poker he'd look up and stare over at me. This is just like being in a romantic film! I laughed to myself as I noticed his eyes fixing on me again.

I'd read a lot in the tabloids about the flamboyant French TV chef. I knew he was a fantastic cook and that he'd just started to hang out on the celebrity scene. Jean-Christophe had become an overnight celebrity after he'd appeared in ITV's *Hell's Kitchen*, and, seeing him for the first time, it was obvious why there was such an appeal. Regardless of his status, though, I was immediately attracted to him. Even from across a crowded room, I'd wanted him to come and chat to me. Even before we spoke, there was an instant chemistry and I knew we were both equally aware of it.

That night I was wearing a pink bra top and a white skirt with slits right up to my thighs. I'd wanted to make an impression at the magazine poker bash and it was certainly working wonders on Jean-Christophe! 'Your eyes are so beautiful and mysterious,' I remember him saying to me in his heavy French accent.

He was standing so close behind me at the bar that when he first spoke I could feel his breath on the small of my neck. My body shook slightly as I turned around and smiled at the handsome face looking at me longingly. I noticed his thick, dark wavy hair, his tanned skin and sexy, deep-set brown eyes. He held out a glass of champagne, which I accepted. 'Thank you so much,' I replied, smiling provocatively. 'Are you enjoying yourself?'

'I wasn't especially enjoying myself until I spotted you,' replied Jean-Christophe flirtatiously, as his gaze wandered down past my neck and then over my cleavage.

As we started to chat, his flirtatiousness and attention was like a breath of fresh air compared to the attention I normally got from the usual footballers and celebrities always out on the circuit. I took a few sips of champagne and quickly decided that I liked this man because he was so different. For one thing, he was French and I loved his heavy accent, plus he had real charisma and certainly no boundaries when it came to being passionate. 'Wow, please give me some warning before you kiss me like that again!' I gasped, unable to catch my breath. Jean-Christophe had suddenly pulled my face towards his and had given me a full-on lingering kiss. It was a sensational kiss, but I wanted the ground to swallow me up because the bar staff and people drinking around us all stopped and stared; it felt like the whole room had frozen. But Jean-Christophe didn't have a care in the world and that was what was so refreshing about him. He always acted on impulse and lived for the moment. If he felt the need for some passion, he just leaped on it.

'Sorry,' he replied. 'I just had to taste you. When I feel chemistry with someone, I need to act on it straight away. I feel such chemistry with you, Cassie.'

I was flattered and I realised that, although he was very forward and that had thrown me, it actually felt nice to be getting some spontaneous affection for a change. This man is different, I thought to myself, as we stood close together and kissed again. I just wanted to experience him. I have to compose myself, I thought. 'I'd love another drink, Jean-Christophe,' I said politely, but what I really needed was time to catch my breath again!

When Jean-Christophe returned with a bottle of

champagne, we moved away from the bar to find a quiet, intimate corner. As we sat and chatted, we kissed again and soon we were completely unaware of anyone around us. I was just happy to be cosied up with him and so when he asked for my number that night I felt so happy.

It was early the next day when my mobile rang. 'Come and see me tonight, darling,' Jean-Christophe whispered sexily down the phone. 'Please come up to Berkshire tonight. I'll cook you something nice and we can spend the evening together at my house. I'll look after you!'

I didn't even have to think about it. For one, I didn't have any plans and, two, I fancied him like mad. 'I'll make my way up to your restaurant by 8pm and we can take it from there. See you later, Jean-Christophe,' I said, and hung up.

Suddenly I felt excitement rush through my whole body. I knew this date was almost certainly going to be purely physical, but it was high time I had some fun! Anyway, Jean-Christophe was too old for me and of course we were worlds apart, but I just couldn't resist him and I didn't see why I should. I hadn't had a date in ages and I needed to be wined and dined, and enjoy a bit of passion. James Hewitt had just been a friend, Russell felt like a million miles away and Celestine even further than that. It's been too long, Cassie, I told myself, as I showered and dressed that morning. I needed to be swept off my feet and romanced by someone I was utterly attracted to, even if it turned out to be just one night.

That evening I dressed casually in jeans and a fitted shirt, but I put on my favourite pair of Christian Dior stilettos. I'd remembered at the party the night before that Jean-Christophe had complimented me on my choice of shoes. I didn't want to let him down that night and of course I specifically chose a French designer! I took the train to Welwyn and then a cab to his restaurant, which was situated in a lavish country house called Brocket Hall. When he came out into the reception area and greeted me, dressed head to toe in chef's whites, I felt excited. He told me that he was busy working, but he smiled and made me feel at home. 'I'll be finished soon, darling,' he murmured, kissing my ear. 'You look stunning, Cassie.'

I sat in the bar just off the restaurant and relaxed. He laid on champagne for me, which was kind, and it actually wasn't that long before he was finished. 'Let's drive back to mine for some dinner. It'll be my treat,' he said gleefully, as we headed into the car park together towards his Land Rover.

'I'd love that,' I replied, as we sped off together.

In the car I could feel the electricity between us starting to build again and it almost reached boiling point when we reached his country house. 'Let me kiss you again now, Cassie. You told me to ask you next time I wanted to kiss you and I am now. Can I kiss you?' he smiled, as we sat in the car in front of his house. We were parked up in his driveway and I was about to get out of the car. Before I could open the door, he pulled me towards him, cupped my face in his hands and then kissed me passionately. It felt amazing, but again, it felt so rushed and so I broke things up and said, 'Let's go inside. I'd love to see your house.'

I'd noticed as we had driven up the driveway that Jean-Christophe had a truly magnificent house. It was very old, but decorated very tastefully. The doorways were so small you had to bend down to get through them. I shivered when I stood in the hallway because as I looked around it felt as if it could be haunted. The low ceilings and beams made it feel so comfortable and warm, though, and I immediately felt at home when I entered. Jean-Christophe took my coat and showed me into his kitchen, which was enormous. I wandered over to the kitchen window and noticed a gorgeous garden, which seemed to go on for miles out at the back.

'Do you want to walk around the garden, Cassie? It's such a beautiful night and we could have a drink together on the veranda before dinner,' he asked.

I agreed, and watched him open a bottle of champagne, get two glasses out of the cupboard and show me out of the kitchen door. The night was heavy and warm. He placed the bottle and glasses on the wooden table on the veranda and suddenly pulled me towards him. By this point I was actually prepared for another of his spontaneous moments, so I relaxed into it and we kissed.

'Do you live here alone?' I coyly asked. I hadn't even thought about that until we were busy kissing one another in the dark on the veranda in his garden. Suddenly it occurred to me that Jean-Christophe couldn't be living in such a huge house alone, plus I'd noticed that it was decorated in a very feminine way. He took a deep breath and then proceeded to tell me that he was single and that he'd been upset because he had split from his wife. 'I'm so sorry, Jean-Christophe,' I said, and wrapped my arms around his waist, hugging him tightly. I hadn't known him long but I hate feeling that someone I know has been hurt; I wanted to comfort him.

He looked down at me. 'I am starting my life all over

again, Cassie. My daughter still lives here which is nice, but I'm devoted to my work now – it's my life. I want to teach as many people as I can in the world how to cook properly and how to really enjoy and savour food. It's a gift I have, and I want to share it,' he explained.

We stood there on the veranda, sipping our champagne and talking about our jobs. I told him about my plans to break into TV and he promised he'd help me with a few contacts. I told him about Papa and he was so surprised. 'How could a father neglect such a beautiful daughter?' he asked, looking shocked. 'Your father should be so proud of having such a beautiful woman for a daughter.'

As I looked out on to the garden I noticed that it was looking so beautiful in the moonlight. There were fairy lights dotted over the top of the veranda and they sparkled like stars.

'Let me show you the garden before it gets too dark,' he suddenly said, grabbing my hand. But it was difficult for me to walk on the grass because my stiletto heels kept sinking into the earth! As we wobbled together down towards the end of the garden, we giggled. We soon reached a fence, where we stopped and Jean-Christophe had to prop me up with his arm. He pointed at the sky and explained which stars we would see, and where they would be if we came back later when the moon was shining properly. I really felt like I was playing a part in a romantic French film!

'Have you ever been with an older man, Cassie?' he asked, looking longingly into my eyes.

'Yes, but not for a long while,' I said, as I remembered Dan in Sheppey and I laughed inside because they were so totally different! Suddenly I felt a million miles away from that time. My body went cold, thinking how much my life had changed. Here I was, taking control of a situation with an older man. It gave me a huge sense of satisfaction, knowing where and who I now was. At that moment in Jean-Christophe's garden I felt powerful. I was in control of this man who stood before me and I knew exactly what I was doing. There would be no tears or feelings of confusion and frustration as I had had with Dan all those years ago when we split up. I wanted to savour the moment and just have fun.

I knew that Jean-Christophe and I would probably end up taking things further that night because we both really found one another irresistible. Even as we stood by the fence in the garden looking at each other and at the sky, it started to get heated. 'I want to make love to you, Cassie,' he said softly. 'Here, on the grass.' And he suddenly tried to pull me towards the ground!

'No,' I said softly. 'I hardly know you, Jean-Christophe.' I pushed him off and I know he was disappointed.

We walked back up to the house in silence. My heels were still digging into the ground and I was wobbling but this time I didn't have his arm to hold on to. I know it must have felt like a rejection to him but we had only been together for half an hour and I certainly wasn't going to jump into bed with him straight away! These Frenchmen move very quickly, I laughed to myself. I wanted to kiss and touch him because he was irresistible, but I needed a bit more time. 'I do like you, Jean-Christophe,' I told him. 'But I would rather take things slowly. I just want to enjoy our evening together and see what happens.'

Despite what I said, after I had declined his advances on

the grass, things were steadily becoming more purposeful. I knew he wasn't relationship material for me but I enjoyed his company and was so attracted to him and he was very wise. Though he was disappointed that we hadn't made love on the grass, he was still charming and when we approached the veranda I was starting to feel tired. 'Let me show you the rest of the house,' he smiled, breaking the silence. And so we clambered up the grand wooden stairs to the top of his house. When we got to his bedroom I started to giggle. There was a huge chart on the wall with his fitness regime written across it for each day of the week. It had the days of the week across the top and then down the side, the exercises he had done that day and the number of minutes he had spent on each exercise. 'I love fitness,' he said, smiling, and I could see that by his excellent physique. 'Obviously!' I laughed and then, while I was busy looking at the chart, Jean-Christophe sat on his bed. I turned back to face him and he suddenly pulled me on to the bed. '*Tu es tres belle, Cassie,*' he said. And I laughed. I did want to make love to him and, although I wouldn't have normally done so on a first date, the sexual attraction was way too much. It doesn't matter, Cassie. You're a grown woman now and sometimes you need to dive in, I told myself, as he took me in his arms. We kissed and cuddled on the bed and it was lovely. The sex was amazing and at one point he started to nibble my skin, starting on my face, down my neck, my arms...

It was an hour later when we stopped and then we lay there together, exhausted. My stomach was rumbling and he noticed. 'I got so carried away with you, Cassie, I forgot to cook!' he exclaimed.

We dressed and headed back down to the kitchen. It was

so sweet, watching Jean-Christophe rustle up a delicious dish of pasta and aubergine for me in his kitchen. The pasta made me feel really sleepy so I told him I needed to rest. He lent me a toothbrush and pyjamas, and we headed back into the bedroom where we slept, wrapped in each other's arms.

The next morning we kissed again in bed and Jean-Christophe made me breakfast. There was a tension between us, but I was happy. 'Is something wrong?' he asked me, as I sat sipping my cappuccino at the huge wooden kitchen table.

'No darling, I just have a lot on. Can you drop me at the station soon?' I asked.

'Sure. When can I see you again?' he asked.

By that point I just wanted to go home, and I avoided answering his question. I'd had a nice and fun experience with Jean-Christophe, but that was it. I'd fancied him and had wanted to enjoy him, but that was all I wanted. I didn't want a boyfriend or to get into a big dating thing because I felt independent and strong on my own. At that time, men weren't a priority for me in any way. An hour later we sat in his car at the station and, after he kissed me on the cheek, we quickly said our goodbyes.

As soon as I got home I stripped off and stepped into the hot shower. As I soaped my arms I noticed bruising all the way down my forearms. I looked at my thighs and they were exactly the same. 'Oh, no!' I laughed. 'He's covered me in love bites!' The problem was that I had a photo shoot that afternoon and knew that I couldn't go with my body and skin in that state. I called up the magazine and cancelled my day with them. It really looked like I'd spent the evening with a vampire! After that week Jean-Christophe called a few times but we couldn't find the time to meet. I then discovered that he had been seeing the actress Patsy Kensit, which made up my mind for me that I didn't want to see him again. I was indifferent to 'us' anyway; I took our night for what it was. I took responsibility for it and didn't have any expectations. I'd had a nice time with him, but I didn't want to complicate my life with anyone. I was in control from start to finish and that felt so great.

It was the same end game with the TV star Ben Freeman. As with Jean-Christophe, I just wanted to have fun with Ben and knew that we wouldn't have a long-term, full-on relationship, but I definitely wouldn't have got involved had I known that he was still busy chasing his ex-girlfriend! It was September 2005 and I'd seen reports in the tabloids that Ben had split up with his *Emmerdale* co-star Amy Nuttall. I wasn't especially interested in him and had never really thought he was sexy or anything. It was just a chance meeting on a random night out; we happened to fancy one another and wanted to share some fun.

The first time we met was when Ben chatted me up on the dance floor at Funky Buddha, a club in the West End. Just as Jean-Christophe had done, Ben picked me out in the room and came over for a chat and a dance. That night we danced for hours and hours together and, as the music got faster, our dancing got sexier and sexier! 'I like the way you move,' he'd said to me earlier that evening and I'd recognised him immediately. It was all so tacky and he had made such a cheesy comment that I cringed a bit. But when he moved nearer to me on the dance floor I actually started to think how attractive he was. He had a handsome, defined face with intense, sparkly eyes. 'Come closer to me then,' I whispered confidently in his ear. Ben and I set to work, grinding and getting closer to one another as the beats picked up a pace.

I was so worn out when the track ended that I was pleased when he asked if I needed a rest and a drink. When we hit the dance floor again after we'd had our drinks, our hands were soon all over each other and it must have looked like we were about to have full sex there! I've always watched *Emmerdale* so I accidentally kept calling him Scott! It was hysterical and, as the drinks flowed, we laughed and laughed together. When the club shut, he suggested going back to his hotel room in South Kensington to carry on drinking. Once there, we just carried on drinking and chatting. Nothing much happened between us because Ben's student brother walked into the room and shouted, 'I'm not watching!' before crashing out on the bed next to us.

It was hysterical because there was Ben, trying to have an intimate chat with me, and his brother had fallen asleep on the bed next to us. In the end we all fell asleep and I felt fine. I knew that Ben and I would go on a date after that night, and that I liked him. 'I'll call you tomorrow, Cassie,' he said, kissing me on the lips when we left the hotel the next morning. But he actually called that night, asking me to meet him as soon as he could get back down to London. I was happy he liked me and was also happy when he started to send me sweet texts every day. 'When I get a break in my film schedule, I'll come down and we can have some fun together. Without my brother, though!' he'd write and I'd reply how I couldn't wait to see him.

The next time he came back down was a few weeks

later. Together, we hit the West End and spent the night at Chinawhite and then returned to the same hotel in South Kensington. Over the previous two weeks, we'd sent loads of sexy texts to each other. We couldn't wait to kiss again and, sure enough, as I sat on the bed in the hotel room, Ben stripped off really quickly and started to kiss me all over. His body was amazing and he was well toned. I didn't mind how he virtually threw me round the bed and at one point we fell off it. I got burns on my bum! Also, his brother didn't disturb us this time so that was great!

After our first proper date, Ben started texting me even more regularly when he got back to Yorkshire. 'This feels great!' I'd tell myself every time he would send me a nice text. I really thought it was becoming a relationship because he would constantly talk about coming down to London to see me again and how he was missing me. But then everything went quiet when I went on holiday to Ibiza for a week. I'd booked my holiday with a friend called Jade from home. It was a well-earned break from work and I just couldn't wait to get out of London and have some fun. Of course, Ben was in the back of my mind when I was there but I knew that when I got back home we would meet up. 'I'll call you when you get back, Cassie. I'll miss you!' he said the night before I'd flown.

'Great, well, you have a good week and can't wait to see you then,' I replied happily.

Ben knew the exact date that I was coming back, but that day came and went and he didn't text. I thought it was strange when I got into bed one night a few days afterwards that I still hadn't heard from him. He's probably busy filming a lot this week. I don't want to bother him. He'll probably call at the weekend, I told myself and drifted off to sleep.

The next day I opened the papers and was gobsmacked. One paper said that Ben had spent the past month getting cosy with his ex-girlfriend Amy! The *People* also ran a story that Ben was seeing both Amy and me. I was shocked because, although we weren't really serious, I thought I was definitely seeing him. I was really disappointed because it felt like there were two parts to his life. He used to say that he worked really long hours and that was why it was difficult for him to come to London and I believed him! Naturally I was upset and, when I read on, the paper said that Ben had been trying to win Amy back. The article said that they had been on a string of dates but all the while he'd been telling me that he wanted to see me again and that the sex we'd had was amazing! If only Amy knew, I thought, and threw the paper in the bin.

I wasn't too upset over Ben because, like I said, we weren't serious and we'd had fun. More than anything, though, I was disappointed because he'd made me look like a fool. He seemed very keen on me and was always texting me and calling me so I was surprised to hear that he was trying to get back with Amy. Still, you live and learn and, just as with Jean-Christophe, I was in control of my feelings and I just moved on. I was having too much fun and enjoying work too much to be bothered by any sort of relationship fiascos or mishaps with men by that stage.

I was a young, single girl, footloose and fancy-free. I didn't really want a boyfriend but I enjoyed dating and being wined and dined. For the first time in my life, I was completely on my own – and I was happy that way.

Chapter Sixteen

Chelsea Games

AFTER THOSE TWO FUN LIAISONS, I REALISED THAT THE
CELEBRITY-DATING SCENE JUST WASN'T 'ME'. I was still keen
to attend celebrity functions and media events, but I
decided that I no longer wanted to mix business with
pleasure. I'd had fun with Jean-Christophe and Ben, but
that was about it; I also knew that I really didn't want to
date another footballer after being hurt by Celestine. But
life often has its own way and I soon ended up falling
unaware into a relationship with a Chelsea reserve. And I
say 'falling' because I hadn't quite made up my mind about
Steve Watt when we went out on our first date together.

Before I met Steve, I was more than happy to be single.
I always think it's a great sign of strength in a woman not
to need to have a boyfriend all the time. I'd felt like that
all those years earlier when I'd split up with Damian and
now I felt the same way again simply because, for me, my
career was much more pressing.

'You're doing really well now, Cassie,' Craig said to me, one Saturday night when we were out enjoying drinks together at the bar in Nobu, Berkeley.

It was October 2005 and it had been a tough week and I wanted to relax. I'd shot on location almost every day. One day I was doing *FHM*, and the next *Loaded*. I'd also started to work with *Playboy*, doing their lingerie campaigns. Then, I'd be taking calls from the press about James, Jean-Christophe and Ben. I'd been spotted out with them by the paparazzi and so had appeared in several of the usual showbiz columns. Luckily, I was a lot more adept at dealing with the press now than I had been when the Prince Harry stories were printed. I was also shooting with an excellent photographer called Jens Wilkholm, who was new to the business and had a real flair for it. Jens had started to syndicate my photos out for me and, as the shots began to appear everywhere, we also made a nice profit from the sales.

'Your name is really getting about now,' said Craig happily that night. 'I think we should celebrate! Let's get some champagne and then have dinner here, Cassie.'

And he was right. My name was often in the papers and the magazines wanted to shoot me more and more. In fact, I was flat out. When we finished our champagne and sat down for dinner in the plush restaurant, I finally felt that I did have something to celebrate. 'Here's to independence and success,' I said to Craig, as we toasted one another across the table.

That night all I'd wanted to do was have dinner with Craig and maybe spend an hour at Embassy after that. When we finished eating we caught a cab and arrived just before 11pm. Because it was early, it wasn't that busy, but I noticed a group of footballers sitting in the VIP section. 'It's Wayne and Carlton, Cassie,' said Craig. 'Shall we go and join them?' he asked, grabbing my elbow.

'Oh, I'm not sure tonight. I just want to have a drink and then leave. I'm so tired, Craig,' I said. But it was too late because Carlton had spotted us and was waving. We wandered over and sat down with them at their table.

Sally wasn't around that night, but I texted her and told her where we were. 'Is Sally coming?' asked one of the players.

'I've just told her we're here,' I replied, and, an hour later, Sally was sitting next to me and getting into the swing of things. I looked over at the bar and thought about maybe getting another drink, but I was feeling more and more tired. 'I have to get some sleep, Craig,' I told him, yawning. 'Do you mind if I leave you with Sally?'

'Of course, babe, I'll ring you tomorrow,' he replied, and with that I called it a night.

I'd already left the club and was in a cab when suddenly I got a call from Craig. 'Are you home already?' he asked excitedly. 'Someone special wants you to call him.'

I was so tired that I couldn't muster up any feelings of excitement. 'Who?' I asked casually.

'Steve Watt, he plays for Chelsea. He's gorgeous and he spotted you tonight. He wants to take you out for dinner,' said Craig.

I knew my agent was still really keen for me to be seen mixing with this crowd of footballers and celebrities and his press-savvy nature always got the better of him! What I hadn't told him was that I was over all that. 'Listen,

Craig, I just want to be single at the moment. I've got more important things to think about,' I stated bluntly. 'I'd rather build up my profile further without needing to be linked to a footballer – I'm doing well in my own right.'

Maybe I was slightly curt with him, but I was tired and sometimes he pushed the wrong buttons at the wrong time. 'I'm sorry – I'm tired. I know what you're getting at, but I'm going to all the right functions and meeting all the right people and it's paying off now,' I continued.

'OK, Cassie, I understand. But what if you like him? Why don't you just have a drink with him and see how you feel?' he asked.

Dating a footballer had helped so many other successful models, but I just didn't want to go down that route, especially if I didn't fancy them. It was late and I wanted to get off the phone. 'OK, sure, what's his number?' I asked nonchalantly.

'I'll text it to you now,' he said, and within seconds my mobile bleeped with Craig's text.

I glanced at Steve's number, switched off my mobile and climbed straight into bed.

The next day I felt better because I'd slept. I decided I needed a day to myself, set about doing the housework and planned to go shopping that afternoon. I ran myself a huge bubble bath and lay in the hot soapy water and relaxed. But my mobile woke me out of my daydream.

'Have you called him yet?' asked Craig, his voice full of anticipation.

'Give me a chance, I'm in the bath relaxing!' I laughed. 'I'll do it this afternoon.' I hung up and decided that maybe I'd text Steve later on when I'd finished my chores.

I had nothing to lose and it would get Craig off my back.

That afternoon I texted Steve. We then started texting one another for the next few days. They were just flirty text messages and Steve seemed pleasant enough, so, when he finally called and suggested a night out, I agreed. Because I didn't know who he was, I thought it would be easier if we went out in a group together. 'How about meeting at Embassy this Saturday night?' I asked him. I knew Sally would definitely come with me and, because Steve was close to several other players like Carlton Cole, meeting up with him when they were all around would be much easier. If we didn't hit it off, at least I'd have them to chat to!

'Sure. Can't wait, Cassie!' he replied and we both agreed to meet in the VIP section that Saturday.

After that call, I didn't even think about the date. I just told Sally to keep the Saturday night free and that was it. I didn't know Steve from Adam, so I didn't have any expectations when I got ready that evening. When Sally and I got to the club, I spotted Carlton and a few other players milling about the bar. I loved spending time with Carlton because he always looked out for me and made me laugh. We edged our way through the throng of revellers and I nudged Carlton.

'You must be Cassie,' said the blond-haired player, standing at Carlton's side. Steve looked younger than me. Blond and blue-eyed, he was handsome, but wasn't anything like the type of man that I would normally go for.

I smiled politely, kissed him on the cheek and then greeted Carlton.

'I still can't place you,' I told Steve, as he ordered me a drink at the bar.

'I'm a reserve – I also don't hang out with these guys too much. But I'm glad I have because I saw you!' Steve grinned.

I sipped my champagne and for the rest of the night we chatted and we actually got on. We ended up having a lot of fun that night and, as the drinks flowed, I didn't want it to end. Steve looked older than he actually was and I was shocked when he told me he was only 20 as I was 22. Normally, I would not date someone younger than me, but we kind of hit it off and I soon got over having a toy boy.

Things between Steve and me were great at the start: we would have a huge amount of fun together, meeting up at the odd club every weekend and going out for nice dinners beforehand. We just partied together or I would go and watch him play football. It was all very calm and casual, and I enjoyed being with him. And so it was at this point in my life that the real football phase began. Without wanting it, I'd fallen into the whole footballer crowd and become a footballer's girlfriend. I never once thought of myself as a WAG and I certainly didn't date Steve because he was a player, but, when the press caught on to the fact that we were an item, it didn't help matters between us because Steve started to feel insecure.

My connection with the Chelsea crowd wasn't purely about Steve and me. Sally and I were spending less time together because Steve was in my life, so naturally she'd started to find her own company elsewhere. I got to know several players quite well through Steve and those relationships were all obviously platonic, plus Sally was also mixing and socialising with various players. On many evenings, she would tell me that a particular player was coming over that night.

Chelsea Games

'That's great, Sal – but make sure you don't get hurt,' I'd warn her. I did worry about Sally. She was going out with several players at once, but she just didn't seem to care. 'I need to let my hair down, Cassie. It's only a game,' she'd say to me whenever I'd try to talk to her about it. I discovered during this period that Sally was such a tough cookie. Rarely did anything affect her.

In her prime, Sally was one of the best models on the circuit. She loved playing the guys at their own game, that's all. It gave her a great sense of satisfaction to know that she was the winner. 'I'm having fun, Cassie. It's just a game and they know it too,' she'd explain. She was the first to admit that, having been in a long relationship, all she wanted now was just to have fun and a sense of freedom again. She was having a great time and that was all that mattered to her. I really think she was actually still hurting from the break-up with her boyfriend and it was her way of telling herself that she didn't care about men. She was trying to prove herself to men and to prove that they wouldn't get the better of her again.

Just as Sally had explained, over time it became clear to me that these players had their own little game going on. Funnily enough, that game was just as tactical off the pitch as on it! Some of the players we encountered when we were out had girlfriends and some (who I won't name) were married, but they still managed to wangle their way into certain glamour girls' beds and enjoy themselves whenever they could, without anyone finding out! These players knew they had struck gold because these particular girls gave them what they wanted and there were never any comebacks; their liaisons would always be kept a secret too.

Cassie Sumner – Loving It

The Hatton Garden flat soon became famous for having footballers around but, for the record, it was never me that invited them! There was a little shop next door to our entrance and the owners and customers must have thought it very strange to see all these expensive, blacked-out chauffeur-driven cars leaving our council flat. If they'd been able to see through the car windows, they would certainly have spotted a Premiership football player. The neighbours in our block must have been shocked. I never assumed that the players would have felt out of place, though – many of them had probably grown up in council flats anyway, so they probably felt at home.

As I watched the constant stream of footballers go in and out of my flat, Steve started to feel more and more insecure. For three months I'd been happy with him, but, because he knew about so many other footballers' girls, he then began to wonder if I was playing the same game. 'Where are you tonight, Cassie?' he'd ask suspiciously if we weren't out together.

'At home,' I'd reply.

'I don't think so,' he'd snap, and the accusations would start again. His insecurity then became constant. 'I saw you in a cab last night. You said you were staying in!' he would rant down the phone most Saturday mornings if I hadn't seen him the night before.

In the end it was too tough for me to handle because I was actually at home in my pyjamas, watching TV with Sally!

One accusation that went on for weeks concerned one particular player, who I won't name. 'I saw you chatting up so-and-so last night,' he'd say, as we lay in bed together

224

most Sunday mornings. The more Steve swore something was going on between us, the more fed up I became. For one, this particular footballer isn't my type and, two, Steve was my boyfriend. I don't have any respect for people who cheat on their partners. No one has the right to inflict that much pain on another person and maybe that's got something to do with my experience of Papa. If you want to see more than one person, then you should just be single, I think. For me, there are three things in life I don't tolerate and those are liars, cheats and thieves. Unfortunately, what I've been lead to believe about many football players is that normally they fit into one or more of those categories.

Meanwhile, I tried to give Steve a chance. I knew that he'd been cheated on before, so I thought that, if I talked that through with him, we might be able to salvage things. If there's been one thing I've learned over the years, though, it's not to drag past relationship experiences into the next. Not every man or woman is the same and, although it's hard, you need to start every new relationship with a fresh and open perspective. I still wanted to show Steve that I was faithful and that he really didn't need to worry. 'Is there anything you need me to do for you to make you feel better? Please don't think every girl is the same as your ex, Steve. It's not healthy,' I'd say, when I knew he was feeling insecure.

'Just promise me that you won't cheat on me,' he'd reply.

But the more chances I gave him, the more he accused me of being unfaithful. He would even send me harsh texts about it and the end that actually drove me into someone else's arms. I wanted to be with Steve, but the constant accusations just wore me down. Through dating him, I'd realised that I actually wanted to be in a relationship again and was ready to settle down, but he was not the one.

Eventually we split up in December 2005 and, although losing Steve hadn't hurt me, when my friendship with Sally suffered, that mattered more. 'I've met someone really special, Cassie,' she said, when she came home one night, grinning from ear to ear.

I'd noticed that the usual footballer crew hadn't been coming round so much. 'That's great, Sally,' I replied. 'Who does he play for?'

'Oh, he's not a footballer! He's a businessman,' she continued.

But I didn't ask her for any details because she didn't seem to want to offer up anything. I'd known that one day she'd outgrow the phase she was in and meet someone special, and sure enough she had. I was happy for her; I really thought she had found someone special and she was keeping it under wraps in case it all went wrong.

Over the next few weeks, Sally was really secretive about her new man. Once or twice a week, she would go out with him but she never told me where they went or what they did. Then one day when I came home from a photo shoot, Sally wasn't in. 'Are you OK, Sal?' I asked, leaving a concerned message on her mobile. 'Please call me and let me know that you're OK.'

But she didn't reply. I thought about calling the police, but, on the third day, she finally texted me: 'I'm in Dubai. I'm on holiday, babe. I'll be back in two weeks' time.'

I was a bit shocked because she hadn't told me that she was going away on holiday, but I just accepted what she said and got on with my week.

Chelsea Games

The reality was that Sally had moved abroad with her man, but she'd not spoken to me about it. She'd suddenly left the flat, and, yes, yet again I felt that a friend had let me down. But this time I didn't let it get to me. Instead, I accepted it and moved on. Natalie had hurt me a year beforehand and so I assumed that, with Sally, I must have been prepared for it. We were close and we got on, but I never relied on her like I'd done with Natalie. It was pretty annoying what she did, though, because when I found out she'd left the country I was suddenly faced with all the bills and covering the rent for both of us, but I didn't crack under the pressure and just carried on. I had enough work coming in anyway.

In the end, but for different reasons, I moved out of my little haven in Hatton Garden. When I closed the front door for the last time, I realised how far I'd come. I was independent, successful and, funnily enough, Steve had actually got me in the mood to date again. I wanted to be wined and dined; I wanted to fall in love because everything else in my life was in order and now I had the time and space for it. I was ready to let a man in, to give something to someone else. Luckily, at this point I did find real love, and my feelings for Michael were enough to make me give up my lovely home. I thought this new man was someone so very special.

Chapter Seventeen

Michael

I'M A FIRM BELIEVER IN THE FIRST CUT BEING THE DEEPEST. I'D ONLY HAD A HANDFUL OF BOYFRIENDS BEFORE I MET AND FELL IN LOVE WITH THE CHELSEA FOOTBALLER MICHAEL ESSIEN. When we parted, splitting with Michael was definitely the toughest break-up for me. The upside was that I pulled through and found a new strength in myself when it came to love, trust and men. I hadn't really challenged this side of my personal life until then, but through the break-up I discovered a much more genuine and satisfying love with my current boyfriend, Lee, and I also learned how to trust a man unconditionally.

I met Michael in January 2006 at Chinawhite. It was a few weeks before Sally left Hatton Garden and just after I'd split up with Steve. That night Sally and I arrived at China's and we spotted Carlton Cole at a table in the VIP section. As usual, Carlton waved us over, so we sat down with him and enjoyed sipping champagne and chatting. I remember noticing a couple of other men who were sitting quietly at the table next to us. They were quite handsome and seemed to know Carlton well, so I assumed they were also footballers. 'This is Michael,' said Carlton, introducing me to one of the men.

'Hi, I'm Cassie,' I replied.

'Pleased to meet you, Cassie,' Michael said, as he fixed his gaze on my face. 'I saw you come in tonight,' he added, kissing my hand.

The club was dimly lit but I noticed straight away that Michael had sexy, deep-brown eyes and a beautiful wide smile. At that point I felt a tremble run down my spine so I pulled my hand away nervously. 'I need to dance, Sally,' I said, flustered. I then hit the dance floor with Sally and another good friend of mine called Shalimar, who'd just joined us.

As the three of us danced, another partygoer started to pester me. 'Cassie, come and sit with me if he's bothering you,' I heard Michael say behind me. I turned round and there he was, smiling at me. He then whispered in my ear, 'He's too much for you. I can see it's troubling you, so come and sit over here with me.'

I felt really relieved that Michael had come over to get me. I didn't want to be near the other man and suddenly felt like I wanted to be near Michael. 'Thanks, you're kind,' I replied, and followed him back to the VIP table.

He placed his hand on a cushion next to him. 'Sit down here, Cassie,' he murmured. 'You'll be fine with me. No one can bother you over here.' So I sat down and relaxed. He poured me a glass of Cristal and told me that he was from

Michael

Ghana and that he'd just arrived in London. 'I love this city!' he exclaimed, then added, 'But I don't know a soul.'

'Well, you know one now!' I laughed. He smiled back at me and then placed his hand over mine. I felt nervous again so I told him that I really needed to go to the ladies'. I stood up and started to wander over to where the queue started.

The club was packed and it was way too hot, but suddenly I felt a firm hand on mine. 'It's really busy in here. Let me escort you to the ladies' and at least I know you're still safe,' Michael said softly, as he walked with me towards the queue. 'I'll wait for you here, Cassie. I don't want you to get lost!' he added, and stood outside the door while I wandered inside.

'Michael's gorgeous, Cassie,' beamed Shalimar. She was already in the ladies', chatting to a few other girls. 'He's a top footballer and seems so nice!' she added, as we powdered our noses together in front of the dimly lit mirrors.

'Sure,' I replied.

As soon as I met Michael I knew that he was different so I didn't want to put him in the same box as any of the other men I'd met, but I didn't want to get close to a footballer again, either. He seemed really sweet and quiet, and wasn't cocky at all. I'd warmed to him, but again he was a footballer and I quickly remembered how vulnerable I'd felt with Celestine and how things hadn't worked out with Steve. When I left the ladies' with Shalimar, I'd already decided to leave it, so, when Michael asked me for my number, I refused to give it to him. He was disappointed, but I needed to be honest with him and, without giving him all the details about Celestine and Steve, I told him that I didn't want to go through the whole dating a footballer thing again. 'I have to leave, I'm afraid,' I told him after that.

'OK, well, I've got training tomorrow, so I'm leaving now too. I'm leaving through the back door. Come with me and I'll get you a cab out there so you're safe,' he said caringly.

At the back door of Chinawhite, we kissed each other on the cheek and that was it. I thought it was polite of him to make sure that I got a cab safely, but when I got home I'd already forgotten about him and soon fell fast asleep.

The next day Carlton called me and told me that Michael liked me and was desperate to get my number.

'I really don't want to date another footballer!' I told Carlton on the phone. But, when he said that Michael wanted to take me out for dinner and that he'd pleaded with him to set it up, I relented. I sat down in the kitchen and thought about Michael. He really seemed different and funnily enough I suddenly felt a tingle of excitement, thinking he might call me. I remembered his eyes and smile, and thought how caring he'd been.

Michael actually rang straight away and after that first conversation we spoke a few times later that week. He was hard work on the phone, though – really shy and quiet, so I had to do most of the talking, which wasn't difficult! But he was also sincere, which I liked and I also got the impression that he thought about me a lot because, after that first phone call, he'd text me every morning with 'Morning, Cassie' and 'Goodnight, sweetheart' each night before I went to sleep. Looking back, I know that I was slowly becoming attached to him because I remember looking forward to his calls and texts every day.

On our first date Michael told me that he was staying

at the Chelsea Hotel because he hadn't found a house yet. He didn't know where I lived so he booked me a cab and asked me to meet him at the hotel. That night I dressed sexily in jeans and a silky top, and jumped into the cab that was waiting for me outside my flat. I felt butterflies as I approached the hotel and was really looking forward to seeing him. 'I'm so pleased you came tonight, Cassie,' he said, as we hugged one another near the hotel reception desk.

I remember that I felt an instant attraction towards Michael. Just as in the club a few nights before, I noticed his amazing eyes and dazzling smile.

'I've booked a table for us in the hotel restaurant, so I would be pleased if you would join me for dinner?' he asked politely. He seemed nervous, but he took my hand and together we went into the restaurant.

It was all very relaxed as we sat chatting and eating together. When the bill finally came, I didn't want the night to end and so I was pleased when Michael asked me if I wanted either to go out dancing with him or watch a movie with him in his hotel suite.

'Let's go to your room and watch a film,' I said happily. Being alone with him in his room would be the perfect end to a perfect night. I didn't want to have sex – I just wanted to be close to him. I can't explain why, but that's what I felt. I trusted that his intentions were good and he seemed such a gentleman so it felt natural for me to want to do that. I'm attracted to an aura that some men have – I suppose it's a kind of charisma and I can tell straight away if I will click with a man both physically and mentally; to me, that's a real turn-on.

After Michael paid the bill, we walked arm in arm up to his room and I remember smiling at him as he lay next to me on the bed. He switched on the TV and we started to watch a film. When the film ended, we kissed, but nothing more. That first kiss was beautiful and sensual; it sent shivers all over my body. It was getting late so I told him I needed to get home. 'Let me drive you, darling,' he said warmly, and added, 'I can then find out how to get to your flat.' My heart skipped a beat because that meant he wanted to see me again! Sure enough, when he stopped the small silver Mercedes outside my flat, he said, 'Cassie, I'd love to see you tomorrow.'

As I shut the car door behind me, I was overjoyed. This man is lovely. He's genuine and caring, and he didn't try to get me into bed, I thought to myself, after kissing him goodbye and agreeing to see him again the next evening. The only negative thing was the communication problem that I'd definitely noticed between us. It wasn't a language barrier, but, as I said before, it was a case of Michael being quiet and shy. As I got to know him better, I discovered that his shyness made it difficult for him to converse with people, but, at the beginning of our love affair, I was happy to overlook it because he made me feel so fantastic and special inside.

The next night Michael came to pick me up himself. I dressed in skinny jeans and knee-high boots and I remember him complimenting me on my fashion sense when I got into his car. Again, we headed over to the Chelsea Hotel where we sat and watched TV together in his suite. Michael had training the next day so I knew that we couldn't go out dancing, which was fine by me! That evening we lay on his bed and couldn't stop kissing each other! It was so passionate but we were just enjoying being together and neither of us gave the other any pressure for anything more. After a few hours of kissing and chatting, I went home again, with Michael dropping me off in his car.

I was so happy because Michael hadn't pushed me for anything more that night – I felt comfortable with him and thought there was something very respectful about him. When I got inside my flat, I called Shalimar. 'Don't, for God's sake sleep with him!' she warned me that night. 'If you like him and he likes you, it shouldn't happen yet anyway.'

I knew she was right because, if I wanted something more permanent with Michael, sex needn't have been an issue at that stage.

It was a month later when we first made love. I'd actually grown to love Michael by that time and it felt so perfect. We were in my flat in Hatton Garden and it happened after I'd made him dinner and we'd settled down in bed. I was so glad that I'd waited because making love that first night with Michael felt amazing! We lay in each other's arms and fell asleep.

After that, Michael and I became really close. When we weren't together, he would text me all the time and I was thrilled that I seemed to be on his mind day and night. It was at this time that he moved to Cobham in Surrey. For him, the move was a positive one because he'd found a proper home and could now settle into life in the UK. The only negative point was that it then became pretty difficult for us to see one another because of the distance between our homes. At first, we dealt with it and Michael would still come and see me or I would get cabs to and from Cobham, but there was at least two hours of travelling almost every other day and it soon started to wear us both out. Despite the constant travelling, we'd also started to settle down together. Neither of us minded staying in and, for me, it was not only because I'd had enough of the party scene but also because, more than anything, I really wanted to get to know Michael. I also wanted him to be more comfortable with me so that he would open up more. I wanted to fall in love and to make sure that side of my life was complete.

Then Michael took things a step further, which made me feel even happier. 'Come and live near me?' he asked one Sunday afternoon when we were sitting watching TV in his living room in Cobham. He was looking at me longingly when he said it and I melted. I didn't even need to think about it because I knew that, if we were to become a serious couple, the distance between our homes would have to change.

'I'd love to,' I replied. 'Let me have a think about Hatton Garden and my work schedule, and then let's talk more and decide on what to do.'

And so he agreed to discuss the logistics of the move and finding a new flat later that week.

It was spring 2006 – Sally had left Hatton Garden and the lease was up on the flat. Perfect timing! I decided to look for a flat in Richmond, which was only ten minutes away from Michael's house. I didn't want to rush things with Michael as the relationship was still young, so by moving to Richmond I would be much nearer but we could still enjoy our own space if we needed to. Then, because I couldn't find a place straight away, Michael offered to help me move my things back to Mum's. I was so excited when he came to help me pack up my things and move from Hatton Garden. It was strange leaving my home because a lot had happened there, but I took comfort in knowing that leaving was another new beginning for me. I was just so pleased that Michael was the one who was part of it.

Michael's house in Cobham was a beautiful four-bedroom house with ensuite bathrooms – a new build, with a huge garden and big black wrought-iron gates. On the top floor was a fantastic cinema room and in the basement there was a garage and a cosy study. Michael used that room as a second sitting room and I'd spend time with him in there playing games on his computer and relaxing. In the end I only stayed there sometimes while I was looking for my own flat, but I got so comfortable there with him that I actually didn't want to go. It was so nice staying with him and waking up with him most mornings.

In fact, my new life with Michael was idyllic. Finally, I was settling down with someone I loved and trusted! I was still working on my career and Michael was also making his mark as a footballer. Even when he went out and I was left alone at his house, it didn't bother me because I knew I'd see him when he came back. He would go to his friend's house a lot and during those afternoons I would catch up with work or call my own friends. It was so comfortable together. I even started to do things around the house for him. If he was away playing football, I'd make sure everything was clean and tidy for when he got back. I'd wash and sort out his football kit and cook him meals. I looked after the garden and anything else that needed attention in his life at home. I was happy to do that and he never took me for granted. It worked so well for us both. I'm quite old-fashioned at heart and I think women should look after their men and that's the role I wanted to play with Michael. At the start it was perfect because I was still able to maintain my career, as well as look after my man.

Regardless of how I felt spending time with Michael in Cobham, I still went ahead with finding my own flat, and Michael helped me with my search. I didn't want to be the one to ask to move in – I wanted him to ask me. Generally, I would never put pressure on a man when it comes to living together and, because Michael never asked me to stay with him permanently, eventually I found a small cosy flat in Richmond and moved in. It was actually nice that I had my own place again, even though I was hardly ever there. I still had some of my things at Michael's house and I'd stay there whenever we were both free. If he was away playing football, I'd go back to my flat and then see him when he returned.

Even though we were becoming more involved, Michael was still quite shy with me, but I actually found that quite endearing and loved him all the more for it. We were like a pair of lovesick kids together most of the time; we'd dance around his house or play games tickling one another in the study. We never really argued and were always laughing. Everyone would constantly comment on how much Michael loved and adored me and he would always be asking me if I loved him because he liked to feel secure with me – and I felt the same.

Michael

'I need you, Cassie,' He'd say every night, as we lay cuddled up in his bed. 'I'm so glad you're here with me – I don't want to be without you,' he'd add and then kiss me goodnight.

I'd always fall asleep feeling like the happiest girl in the world because I was ready to let someone in again.

Chapter Eighteen

A Wag's World

LOOKING BACK, THE FIRST SIX MONTHS OF MY RELATION-SHIP WITH MICHAEL WAS ONE OF THE HAPPIEST TIMES IN MY LIFE. Summertime always gives me a buzz anyway, but I felt even more excited and loved when I grew closer to him. I was thriving because I felt so content and because of this feeling I decided that I wanted to give everything to this man. Around this time I completely changed my life for him.

I remember my daily routine was relaxed and balanced. I felt so content dozing happily in his king-sized bed under the soft white sheets every morning. If I was at his house we'd wake up together around 9am and Michael would then set off for training. I'd reach for the remote control, raise the electronic blinds and watch the sun stream on to the glossy marble floor. I'd always feel a rush of happiness when I'd spot my clothes from the night before draped over the sofa. We'd always make love together and, as Michael tore off my clothes, the sex always felt fantastic.

Often the phone would wake me from my delicious daydreams. 'I'll be down in a minute, Fanny,' I'd tell the cleaner, and then I'd get up from the bed. I'd put on my silk dressing gown and walk down the exquisite spiral staircase to the front door. 'Hi, darling,' I'd say, letting her in. 'I overslept, sorry! Just get on with what you need to.'

I'd then wander through the silver-gilt glass doors and into the living room, thinking about my day ahead. Normally I needed to go to the gym, where I spent an hour with my personal trainer. I'd then have to get to the beauty salon for a manicure and bikini wax, then back home in time to shower, prepare some food and wait for Michael so we could have lunch together. After lunch we normally either went shopping in Knightsbridge or would relax together at home before heading out for dinner or a party in the West End.

Without consciously thinking about it, I'd become a WAG. A typical WAG is someone who is married or dating a footballer and who tends not to have a career of her own (though there are exceptions to this, of course, and I take my hat off to those who forge their own path regardless of their partner's career and income). They have a huge disposable income and they spend a lot of time shopping, having beauty treatments, lunching with friends, attending celebrity parties and looking after their partners. The latter aspect is the most time-consuming and actually a full-time job. The footballer needs to be a WAG's priority if she's going to make him happy and their relationship is to be a real lasting success. Because I have now experienced true WAGdom, I take my hat off to those WAGs who somehow manage to cut it and continue to keep their partners happy.

Despite becoming a WAG, I never really mixed with any of the other WAGs until I started filming *WAGs Boutique* in November 2007. It was then that I made some fantastic friends. But, before that exciting period in my life, I never socialised with any of the Chelsea wives and girlfriends, even though Michael played for Chelsea, because they were way too competitive. I remember vividly my first Chelsea game. I'd decided to sit in the friends and family section and spotted Toni Poole (who was engaged to John Terry) and Elen Rives (Frank Lampard's wife) in the players' box. They caught my eye straight away because they were decked out in Gucci, their faces covered with huge sunglasses. Their lives are slightly ridiculous, I thought to myself as they sat chatting, ignoring the exciting game that was unfolding in front of them. There they were, dressed up in Gucci at Stamford Bridge in the driving rain! It seemed to me as if it was all about the way they looked, rather than the important match that day.

I did often enjoy the WAG routine, though – like I'd lunch with my girlfriends at The Conrad and then head off with them to a game, but I never hung out with the other girls before, during or after for a match. Saying that, I have my own friends and I'm not really the kind of person to make lots of new friends anyway. Maybe I'm like this because I've been turned over one too many times. I assume some people might find me rude or think I don't like them, but I think that I'm a typical Capricorn in that respect: cautious and reserved.

Regardless of the feelings I had about the other Chelsea WAGs, at the start of our time together, I was just content to make Michael happy. Of course, the luxurious lifestyle that I now had was a bonus, but it was the love I had for and from Michael that really mattered to me. Michael loved me and I him, so naturally I wanted my world to revolve around him.

As I said, I thrived on making Michael happy, so, even when I spent time on myself at the beauty salon or spent money shopping in town, it was purely to make him feel proud of me and to keep him happy. What girl wouldn't want to look the best she possibly could for her boyfriend? What's more, being a WAG meant you had to look your best, especially with all those other women eyeing up your man! Most mornings after I'd let Fanny in, I'd pick up any cash Michael had left me on the kitchen table and then dial the beauty salon. 'Hi, it's Cassie, Michael's girlfriend. I need to check the times of my manicure and waxing appointment today and to see if you can also slot me in for a wash and blow dry,' I'd say to my regular beautician. After I moved to Richmond, I never washed my own hair. Looking back, it seems so ridiculous now that three times a week I *paid* for my hair to be washed and dried! If I had time, I would also fit in a waxing, pedicure, spray tan, massage and facials whenever I needed them. You can do all those things yourself or not at all, but if you have money then naturally you get someone else to do them! Anyway, I always had to look my best, especially if a players' party was on because I always wanted to do Michael proud.

In return, he looked after me, mentally and financially. If

I needed anything, I knew I could have it. It made him happy that I was living nearby and I'd moved there mainly because he wanted me near him and at the start it worked and we were very happy together. I had enough clothes from modeling, but Michael definitely wanted me to look nice so I would shop at Gucci and Prada. Money just wasn't an issue for him. He splashed out on a Porsche, which I drove when I wanted to in exactly the same way. It was the lifestyle that he was used to, and he naturally wanted to share it with me, his girlfriend. If I felt good, then he did, and vice versa.

Michael never asked what I spent the money on, but he would always tell me I looked nice, so I knew it mattered to him. It gave him peace of mind to know that everything was being looked after properly by me because I was the one who knew exactly how to keep things running smoothly for him and I was the one who kept him happy.

I was really excited when I went to watch him play for Ghana against America that year. Not only would I see him and watch him play, but I also knew that I would have a great time. A few days after he left, I opened my email to check on the flight times. I smiled to myself, and ran upstairs to pack my suitcase.

When I arrived at the airport, I realised that the trip would be extremely lavish. 'If there is anything you need, Madam, please let us know,' the airport assistant said, as she saw to my every need. The staff at Gatwick knew that I was a WAG and therefore I was given the best service. That afternoon I sat sipping champagne and eating canapés in a private lounge, and I hadn't even had to queue through Passport Control or Security. The two-hour flight was sheer luxury as I was offered a four-course meal and massages and then, after we had landed, I was escorted off the plane by the flight attendants. At Frankfurt Airport, I was driven to the most expensive hotel in a blacked-out limousine. I had a wonderful time on that trip and gave Michael all the love and support he needed in Germany so that he performed the best he could on the pitch.

When we returned home, we flew club class together to Monaco and spent the weekend relaxing and shopping. I remember that, whenever I saw something I liked, Michael bought it for me. During that trip we also drove in a convertible to St Tropez for a few nights. I felt so happy as we sped along the French Riviera with the wind rushing through my hair while we listened to the Fugees on the expensive, built-in sound system. Once there, we booked ourselves into the resort's most exclusive hotel and then headed out into the town. We went to a party in Jimmy's nightclub, which, as I mentioned before, was highly glamorous. I felt like royalty as Michael introduced me to all his old teammates from Lyon, partying there with him that night.

Back in London whenever Michael and I went out, everything was paid for on his debit card and we only went to the most expensive of places. Sometimes I'd get frustrated with him because he'd foot the table bills for us, plus all his friends when we partied at places like Embassy or Mo*vida in the West End. Sometimes the table bill would amount to £7,000 as our guests had polished off copious amounts of Cristal and the best vodka. 'You can't support everyone, Michael,' I'd often tell him on the way home.

'It's fine, Cassie. These are my friends and I want everyone to have a good time when we're all out together,' he'd reply.

But that was Michael. He was generous with the people he cared about, and that was what was so lovely about him. In his mind, what was his was also mine, and that made me feel happy. He didn't care about money or what things cost so long as everyone, including me, was happy.

At the start this seemingly amazing lifestyle was appealing to me, but by the autumn I realised that unfortunately it all came at a price. Footballers are a different entity and living with Michael was sometimes tough because of his expectations of me. Understandably, a footballer's expectation is high because he is treated like a god. At work, everyone looks up to him and rallies round him, and, if that's not happening at home, then he can't deal with it and his home life won't work for him. The club pampers and nurtures their players, and they need their women to do the same.

Footballers have everything done for them by their clubs and, to an outsider like me, it seems they live in a ball of cotton wool. They have someone to organise their finances, their holidays and their home life. If Michael needed anything at all to get through his day, then Chelsea Football Club would arrange it for him. For this reason, someone like Michael will never experience living in the real world. Michael never knew normality in England because he'd shot to the heights of football acclaim at a young age. At work everything was done for him and at home it was the same, and that's where I fitted in. He couldn't cook, clean or look after himself, but it was normal for him to exist like this. Footballers want a woman who can stay at home and support them in every way. They need their women to go to matches, take the kids everywhere and look after their lives.

On top of the practical side of running Michael's life, there was the mental effort I also needed to put in. If Michael won a match, everything was fine. However, if he lost, then he'd watch the game on TV afterwards and mope about at home all weekend. He was so miserable during those times, although Chelsea never lost that much! At one point he was injured and that was the worst time for us. For weeks, he was unable to play and felt so frustrated. 'Don't worry, darling,' I'd say to him, and try to hug him. But my words always fell on deaf ears and he would lock himself away and not want to talk to me. It was frustrating because I knew that all he was thinking about was his football and he'd forget about me altogether. At first, I accepted it and did my best during these times, but gradually the situation wore a bit thin and I started to feel alone. Footballers can't go out when they're training hard and then they can't go out when they're about to play. After a match there was always time for the team to go out together and they wouldn't want their partners there. We'd go for dinner in Cobham together or we would have dinner at home before he headed out with his friends, but most of the time I felt excluded.

One afternoon in October 2006, I remember walking along Sloane Street and staring through the glass windows at all the stylish, expensive clothes. Once they'd all been so mouth-watering, but now I'd actually become tired of it all. I'm so bored of shopping, I thought, as I looked at a pair of stilettos in the Gucci window. I'd have died for a pair of shoes like that two years ago, I thought sadly. Then I went and sat in my car and buried my face in my hands. I started to sob over the steering wheel. I can't do this any more, I told myself. I want my life and career back. You see, women love shopping because it's a treat, and now I could do it whenever I wanted and spend as much as I liked, so it was no longer a thrill, but a chore instead. The days I spent looking for outfits for a night out had become so boring. I couldn't even be bothered to dress myself up to go shopping. Normally, if you didn't dress properly the shop assistants would make you feel uncomfortable, but by that time I really didn't care if they spoke down to me as they eyed up my scruffy tracksuit and scraped-back hair. I had started to hate the whole WAG world and its pretensions, and I wanted to change what was happening around me.

As I said earlier, by that time I'd changed my life for Michael. I'd put my career on the backburner to stay with him because I knew that if I wanted to be with him then he needed my all. For the first few months of our relationship I did work, but gradually Michael started to need more of me and he also didn't want me to work. His career always came before mine and that was never going to change. In my mind, I knew this would have been fine if we were married or engaged, or had kids, but that wasn't the case. By the October I'd also started to worry that if he left me I'd have nothing. I loved Michael deeply, but over time I couldn't see him giving me any more commitment because of his career and his age. And so, after nine months together, I got to a point where I had to take control of my own security and that was in the form of my career.

249

'I feel like I've given up everything for Michael, Mum, but I don't feel fulfilled. I need to work again and I need something more from him,' I said to her on the phone one night.

Michael had gone out to a club in London and I was at home dreading the next few hours. I didn't have anything to do. Michael wanted me there in the morning when he got back and I felt I had to be there because I owed him all the time. I realised I hated not having my own career; also, I thought it was unfair that we were a couple, but Michael had his job and was being put on a pedestal while I wasn't appreciated and I couldn't have mine. I wanted to do something good, like I used to and come home and talk about it. I didn't want to come home and say, 'Look at my new dress or my new nails!', and I didn't want it to be all about Michael any more.

I'm old-fashioned at heart and believe that women should support their husbands, so, if you are married and with kids, then sure. 'We aren't married, Mum,' I told her. 'So things need to change. If I'm giving up so much for someone, then I need to know he will always support me for the rest of my life. What happens if we split up and then my career has completely vanished?'

She knew what I meant because she remembered what she'd gone through with Papa. She'd given up everything for him and her family, yet in the end the support wasn't there and she was unhappy so she'd left. Plus, she naturally worried about me and wanted me to do whatever would make me happy. 'If you don't make a change when you're unhappy, Cassie, you'll regret it for the rest of you life. You need to be happy within yourself before you can make someone else happy, too. I think you need to talk to Michael and iron it all out. You two can find a balance together, I'm sure,' she advised me warmly.

So once again I needed to take control of my life. I decided that I wanted to work again, but I would also try hard to keep Michael happy at the same time. Sadly, even though Michael agreed for me to work again, in his eyes, combining the two just wasn't possible.

Chapter Nineteen

WAGs Boutique

AFTER MY NEGATIVE FEELINGS ABOUT MICHAEL AND MY LIFESTYLE SURFACED, DURING THE WEEKS AFTERWARDS, I SPENT A LOT OF TIME CONSIDERING MY WORK STRATEGY. I knew there were a lot of new management companies out there and so I decided to look at all the options. I spent hours calling some of my old friends in the industry and told them I wanted to model again. Things had not worked out between my manager, Craig, and I and we had parted on not the best of terms – and so I decided to see if there was another manager more suitable for me at that stage. I'd already set up a few photo shoots with some of my old model agents, but I really wanted a new manager. It had worked well before for me. 'There's a new woman working with girls like you, Cassie,' my friend Nicola McLean told me one night. 'She knows all about footballers and press, so she'd be a great start. I'll pass on your number tomorrow for you.'

And she was right because Chrissie Davis landed me my first proper TV gig.

Chrissie was married to a footballer so she really knew the score. We met up for lunch and I told her that, if she wanted to take me on, she'd have to focus on the TV side of things, but I still wanted to model. 'No problem, Cassie,' she said. 'The way it works with me is that I take 20 per cent of all the work I get for you – the rest is yours.'

It all made sense to me so when we parted I felt quite positive about joining up with her. I even told Michael about it when I went round to his house that night and he seemed pleased. Despite his initial response to my working again, however, things changed unexpectedly at home and our relationship took a turn for the worse.

One night we'd finished having dinner together and Michael seemed distracted. I'd noticed that during the meal he was restless and had got up a few times to stand by the kitchen window. 'What's wrong, Michael?' I asked, looking concerned.

After a long silence, he said, 'Cassie, my mum is coming to visit next week. I'm sorry, but you'll have to make yourself scarce for a while.'

His words felt like a knife in my heart. I couldn't understand what he was getting at – it would have meant the world to me to meet his mother. After all, that's what couples do when they're in love. 'Why?' I stammered.

'Because Mum is really sensitive about me having girl-friends and I need to take things slowly with her,' he explained.

But what he was asking me to do only made me feel that I must be an embarrassment to him. He should be proud of me and want to show me off to his family, I thought, as the anger welled up inside of me. I'd had no issues with introducing Michael to my family – they had met on a number of occasions and my youngest brother, Conor, had even stayed with us in Cobham during one of his half-term holidays.

I felt so uneasy about what he'd asked me to do that I got up from the kitchen table, went straight upstairs and packed my things. I don't want to be in the house with him anyway, I told myself, as the tears flooded down my cheeks. I must be missing something here! I then rushed downstairs with my bag and walked back into the kitchen. 'If you don't want me here next week, then I'm going back to my flat right now!' I spluttered. Michael turned towards me and tried to hug me, but it wasn't going to wash. I pushed him off, fled the house and drove straight back to my flat in Richmond.

For two days I ignored Michael's calls and just cried. In my heart, I knew that it wasn't normal to be in a relationship like that. If Michael really loved me, then his family should naturally have accepted me. I was such a huge part of his life but it felt like he'd wanted to keep me a secret. Michael should want me to get to know them, I thought over and over. Nothing else should matter apart from us. And so I decided that I needed a break from him. I spent the days thinking alone in my flat and realised that often I'd felt excluded from Michael's life in other ways – this wasn't just about his mother. He never wanted to be photographed in public with me and I didn't know any of the friends he had made while he'd been out partying. By the end of the second day, I felt certain that I was his secret and that he didn't love me as I'd thought. In the end, I knew it was only a matter of time before we broke up because I certainly couldn't stay with a man who wanted to hide me from the world.

It was the first of many rows that month, October 2006. A few days later, Michael came round and tried hard to make amends. By that point, I couldn't be bothered to argue and wanted so much to give him the benefit of the doubt, so we made up and I got on with my day.

I decided that the week that Michael's mother was there I'd start looking for more work. In fact, the whole scene over his mother just made me more determined to get back into it again. On the Monday I started calling the modelling agencies and then I contacted Chrissie again and she said she'd been busy working on my profile. 'I need you to work harder,' I told her aggressively, that afternoon. 'Get me whatever you can: modelling, TV work, anything! I just want to get my life and career back on track.' I knew I needed to be more assertive and, because I felt anger towards Michael, my drive and determination to get back out there was stronger than ever.

That same month, out of the blue, ITV got in touch with Chrissie. They explained that they had developed a new and exciting programme concept and they wanted *me* to feature in it! I was so excited when she called me about it because, for once in my life, I'd been given a break and I hadn't even been back in the business for five minutes. I knew part of it was down to fate and something was telling me that now it really was time for 'me', but I also knew that some of it was down to me because I'd pushed things as best I could with her.

It was on the following Friday that I met the TV

producers at the Talkback Thames offices in London. 'Are you dating Michael? Can you act up in front of the camera? What do you know about fashion?' The questions were relentless and the production team certainly gave me a grilling that day. I didn't care, though, because it was satisfying to be challenged by something other than driving to the beauty salon or navigating my way up Sloane Street every afternoon!

I spent the weekend alone, biting my nails and waiting for a phone call. On the Monday Chrissie finally called me and told me they were offering me £20,000 in instalments. I jumped with joy, hopped into my car and met her in town to sign the contracts.

My hand shook as I signed my name along the dotted line. 'Well done, Cassie! Let's go and celebrate!' exclaimed Chrissie. It'd been a rollercoaster weekend, but finally I'd decided to take the plunge. I'd just signed up for a brand-new reality TV show called *WAGs Boutique*. This was a charity show and a team game, where two boutiques in London's Soho battle it out to see which one can sell the most clothes. The contestants were real footballers' wives or girlfriends: there would be one overall winner and then one of the shops would win too. It sounded fantastic – fun, lively and just up my street.

The next day I couldn't wait to tell Michael. 'Michael, Michael,' I called up the stairs as I entered his house. 'I've got some great news!' I ran up the stairs to the bedroom, where he was lying half asleep on the bed. He was watching a cartoon but he didn't even take his eyes off the screen to speak to me. 'I got a part in a TV show!' I exclaimed, and sat on the bed next to him.

'That's great, darling. You do whatever you need to. I'll help you in whatever way you need,' he said. With that, he got up, switched off the TV and went into the bathroom.

As I heard the door shut, I bowed my head. He'd already turned on the shower so I knew he wouldn't be coming back out for a while. I sighed, left his house and drove straight to Chrissie's. I needed to talk to her because I knew the show depended on me being with him and, although he'd said he'd support me, in my heart I knew he didn't seem interested. As Chrissie and I talked over a cup of tea, the happiness I'd felt when I'd signed the contract subsided and fear started to well up inside me.

'What about Michael?' I asked Chrissie anxiously. 'I think he might change his mind about me and not want me to do the show.'

'He'll be fine, sweetheart. He'll support you all the way, just like you've done for him with his football career,' she said calmly.

In my heart I knew she was wrong and that, although Michael had agreed that I should do it, his support wouldn't last.

The next week, I was dealt another blow. It was November 2006, and when I read the words splashed across the tabloid I broke down in the kitchen. Michael's mum had flown back to Ghana and I'd had a call from a tabloid the day before asking for a comment about a kiss-and-tell to be published the following day. At first, I'd ignored it, but on the Sunday when Michael was out playing football, I went out and bought the paper and read it in complete despair. It all seemed so true. I hadn't seen him the whole week and, although things weren't back to normal between us, we'd enjoyed a Saturday night watching DVDs and snuggling up on the sofa together.

'What's this, Michael?' I cried, holding out the newspaper so that he could see the front page. He had just arrived home and was walking up the stairs to shower when I confronted him. 'Who is this woman?' I asked, as the tears rolled down my cheeks. I couldn't stop crying and, as I looked over the article, I felt anger. It said that the girl in the story was his girlfriend, but the most awful thing of all was that she said that I wasn't!

Michael stood there in silence. After a while he snatched the paper out of my hands and threw it in the bin. 'It's all lies, Cassie,' he said, putting his arms around me. 'That's why I don't get involved with the press. It's just not part of my life or what I want to do. You need to ignore it because I never slept with her.'

He went on to explain how he knew the girl (Lureta), but, according to him, nothing had happened. I calmed down when he sat there, telling me why he thought that she had sold the story. 'We flirted one night, Cassie, but that was it. She probably wanted more and felt angry because I wouldn't give it to her. I love you, and that's what matters, not some silly tabloid story.'

That morning he pleaded with me to believe him. I didn't know what to believe, though: the paper had made me look bad and that upset me because I hadn't done anything. I sat on the floor and cried, with Michael sitting beside me. Deep down, I still didn't know if he was telling me the truth and somehow I knew that things between us were going from bad to worse.

When I started doing *WAGs Boutique*, I was filled with

excitement, not only because I could get my teeth stuck into something new, but also because I'd always loved being surrounded by clothes and fashion. The whole idea of opening a shop and starting from scratch was also very appealing and it sounded challenging because I knew I'd also gain business experience, something I'd never had before.

At the start, the only worry I had was about the other WAGs. There were ten of us altogether: Jadene Bircham, Madeleine Bowden, Michaela Henderson-Thynne, Elle Isaac, Charlotte Mears, Julie Phillips, Krystell Sidwell, Heather Swan, Nichola T and myself. Up until then, I'd deliberately chosen not to be part of the WAG crowd; that scene just wasn't me, I thought. Funnily enough, the girls on the show proved me wrong and, although they're WAGs, they're some of the nicest girls I've ever met and many of them are still good friends.

The filming schedule was different from when the shop officially opened in February 2007. From November 2006, I worked extremely long hours, often having to get up at 6am and not getting home till gone midnight. We were opening in less than three months and we had to set the business up from scratch. We were split into two teams, each with a mentor, and we then began to run our very own business. My team, 'Better Half', had to do everything, from choosing the shop name to buying all the stock and then designing the fixtures and fittings. And all this had to be filmed because those jobs were part of our tasks, later aired on TV!

We knew the competition from the other shop, 'Bows', would be tough and so we threw ourselves, heart and soul, into making our boutique as fashionable and trendy as we could. Because everyone knew I had a flair for fashion and was a model, I did the majority of the buying for my shop, but I worked alongside Heather and Charlotte. The three of us loved fashion and had different knowledge and tastes to offer into the mix and it worked because we produced some great outfits. Funnily enough, my mentor, Lyn Gardner, told me that I had a natural aptitude. I had to travel to Paris at the start of the show to do all the buying, which was great. I love Paris and I love shopping, but it was extremely hard work because we were only there for three days and we had to fit in as many viewings with fashion houses as possible. One day, I remember oversleeping, though, and missing two interviews. I think I'd had too many Margaritas at the plush hotel bar the night before!

When we finally opened the boutiques, each WAG had a go at everything: selling, managing, assisting and going out on buying trips. Each week, we also had to work through specific fashion challenges created by the production team and geared around fashion. For example, we had to design an advert using the name of our shop for the promotional challenge and we had to design our own red carpet dress for a celebrity and then get it made. On top of this, we had to make sure our shop was selling the most stock. That meant choosing the right clothes, pricing them properly and finding out what sold the fastest.

I think I was a good manager and I would have liked to be the manager full time! I really loved the fashion side and making creations for the general public to see. For the first time in my career I had such a good response from the public and, even to this day, I get so much support from

261

my fans, which is great. The best thing was that I really enjoyed learning to work as part of a team. I loved the girls and we would have such a laugh together, especially Charlotte and me. But I disliked the long hours as I'm quite a social person and I had very limited time for my friends, plus I didn't enjoy the selling very much because I'm not that pushy and I couldn't lie to girls who looked awful in leggings and flounced tops! I also hated being told off by the other girls when they were managing, because I'm used to being my own boss and doing what I want, when I want!

When the shop finally opened, we started to work normal shop hours. We had to open at 10am and close at 6pm, but it was still demanding because again we were being constantly filmed. The shop was open from Wednesday to Saturday, and then on Sundays we had to film interviews to discuss the week's happenings and the results of the challenges, and talk about the next week's challenges. Each day was different and some of them were tough, mainly when I had to deal with difficult customers. On one occasion, I had an argument with a customer because she'd started insulting me and the other girls by saying the stock was overpriced and that we had more money than sense! It really infuriated me because the proceeds were all going to charity. In the end, I told her to leave. After all, we were doing the show for charity and she'd made it sound as though we were doing it to line our own pockets! Yes, we were paid a fee for participating, but all of the profit from the shop went to charity.

The only other big argument was with Jadene. We were doing a Radio 5 Live interview with Gabby Logan and everyone was aware that no one was to talk about my situation with Michael because it was still very upsetting for me. I had also given the exclusive to *OK! Magazine*. But Jadene raised the issue and Gabby was very cutting about it all. I was really upset and so I talked her down. After the interview Jadene started criticising me in front of everyone for embarrassing *her* live on radio! I was so embarrassed and upset at her actions and I thought she was being very insensitive. After that, our friendship never recovered. I think I bickered with all the girls at some point, but I can honestly say that mostly we all got on well together and had such a laugh. We spent so much time together, we really became like a little family.

It was also fantastic because I received loads of fan mail when I was in the shop. I loved Valentine's Day that year because I think I received something like thirty cards! The best fan mail was from a little girl, saying she really admired me. She sent me a gorgeous necklace that I have kept: it has a pretty little butterfly on it. Apart from this, all sorts of people came in the shop so that was fascinating. We had a group of drag queens, so extrovert and funny! I loved them and had never met people like them before.

When the show wrapped after three months, Charlotte was the overall winner and 'Bows' won the team effort. I was disappointed, but we had done our best – it really had been a battle of the tills! But it was down to the public to decide who was voted Queen of the WAGs and Charlotte deserved that crown!

We had the wrap party at Aura, where there was a free bar, and so we all let our hair down and got sloshed! Everyone was there, from production to family and friends, so it was great to finally relax together, although a little sad to have to say our goodbyes.

Doing the show definitely gave me a taste for fashion and business. I'd love to do some kind of work in the fashion world again, although I can imagine it's very cut-throat. Anyway, I think I've battled through that sort of aggression in the modelling world so I know I'd survive.

Doing *WAGs Boutique* was the final nail in the coffin for Michael and me. The worst thing was that at first he was all for it and even agreed to do an interview. Actually, I felt hopeful that the show might make things better between us and that he'd be proud of me. I'd come to terms with the situation with his mum and had tried to forget the kiss-and-tell – I just wanted us to move on together. For me, doing the show seemed like a brand-new start when we began filming.

However, after I signed the contract and started the show, things between us were strained. When I had some time off from filming before the launch of the shop, I realised that Michael and I would never recover. I fell out of love with him because he rarely asked me about the work I was doing, although he knew full well that I was in my element. He started complaining that I wasn't around since I'd started filming that November, but the schedule was tough. Doing the show meant we had to fly to Paris to buy stock and I was away a lot, but I was out there again doing something with my life and had met a great group of girls. Each day when I woke up, I felt excited because at last I was getting my teeth into something. I enjoyed being out there and doing something other than shopping and getting my nails done.

Because Michael was quite private and never courted

publicity, I was clear with the production team that it needed to stay that way. 'Don't worry,' the production assistant said reassuringly. 'We'll clear everything with his agent and work closely with them.'

I felt relieved that they were being so understanding and called him straight away to fill him in about the potential interview I needed him to do.

'No worries, Cassie,' he said. 'I'll chat over it with you tomorrow. If they can send the questions to my agent, that'd be helpful.'

But the next day we never did chat because Michael suddenly pulled out without telling me. 'Apparently he has changed his mind, Cassie. I'm sorry,' said the assistant on the phone. 'He won't get involved.'

I was gob-smacked, and I knew I would have to go on TV and say I was Ms Michael Essien, but I'd told Michael all the details from the start. By then, I'd already started filming but I knew from what the assistant said that Michael was now going to make things difficult for me.

I drove straight over to his house and confronted him. 'Why didn't you tell me?' I asked, sobbing. 'We can always talk through things together and you had agreed to do the show, Michael! This is potentially harmful for my career.' I was furious with him, but he just wasn't interested.

'I don't want to get involved, Cassie. You aren't spending any time with me any more and me supporting that show would mean me supporting us not being together,' he said.

After he said that, I was fuming even more because I knew he was using the relationship breakdown as an excuse. Sure, I was busy, but why couldn't I work?

That day, Michael tried his hardest to persuade me to pull out. 'I look after you, Cassie – you don't need to work,' he said. But when he looked at me he knew that I wouldn't give in: quite rightly, the show had taken his place. By this point, we were relatively apart anyway and would speak on the phone most days, but it would be tense. I would have to call him after receiving phone calls from the estate agents. Sadly, we were both preparing ourselves for the inevitable break-up.

The week before we split I woke up and drove to his house. I have to confront this, I told myself in the car. Something isn't right. When I got there, I couldn't find Michael. I walked into the study and noticed that on his laptop was a screensaver of another girl. Usually there were pictures of me on there and he would stare at it for hours, which always made me feel special. Upset, I called his mobile. 'What's going on?' I shouted at him. 'Who's the girl on your screensaver?'

'She's no one – I just found that shot on the Internet, so I swapped it with yours,' he replied.

I looked around the study and then spotted a photo of him and a girl hugging one another in a frame on the wall. 'Who's the girl in the picture frame then?' I asked.

'Oh that's someone from church,' he replied.

It was so hurtful because he knew full well that I would see the pictures when I went in there. They were both in full view! I felt sick and hung up: it was all getting too much for me.

In the end the kiss-and-tell, his mother and then Michael deciding to back out of the show made me realise he didn't want me any more. A week before my birthday we split up for good. 'Are you sure you want us to break up?' he said.

'Yes,' I simply replied.

Michael cried a lot and he kept saying, 'In a couple of months once things have sorted themselves out, we could get back together, Cassie.'

But I knew that if we split there was no going back: I was ready to go. We weren't having sex or even talking and, most of the time, I didn't know where he was.

That day I really thought we'd split maturely and amicably. The show was being aired in two days so, when I told the producers that things had ended between us, they told me the show had already gone too far and they wanted to keep me in it. Then Michael shocked me to the core. He left angry calls on my phone and issued a statement the day before the show was to be aired. That statement said clearly that I wasn't his girlfriend and that I was just a friend. I took what he was saying to mean that we had only ever been casual acquaintances and this really did upset me.

I thought that statement would sabotage my role in the show but luckily someone up there was looking out for me. What Michael did to me still hurts – he should have just let it go and allowed me to enjoy my success. Even now people still think I lied, but it wasn't like that at all. I was honest and told the producers about the split, but they said that, once the first show had aired, they would cover the split in the second. Yes, we had split up, but at the time I was mortified when Michael didn't even call me to explain or answer my calls.

Every time I think about Michael it still hurts. For a year I'd done everything for him and put him first. I'd never stepped out of line with him. But I didn't have time to mourn him and as I got into working on the show I felt lonely at night without him. For a while, I stayed in the flat in Richmond until the phone was cut off and then ceased all contact. He seemed to want nothing to do with me. Despite this, I just carried on regardless and brushed all my feelings under the carpet, throwing myself into work.

For the first time in a year I was earning, although it was hard work and I worked every hour under the sun to make the show a success. Often we filmed into the night and then I did press and my other modelling engagements when I could so, as you can imagine, I was flat out. Sometimes, when I got home and I felt tired, I would cry myself to sleep, but the next day I'd get up and do it all again. I was back working and that was all that mattered. I got on with the girls and they were really supportive, just like a family, and that support when I lost Michael is what really made a difference to me.

Chapter Twenty

Finally Me

IN MARCH 2007, I FINISHED WAGS BOUTIQUE AND I FELT EXHAUSTED. Although I'd thoroughly enjoyed working on the show, the back-to-back filming had been gruelling and it had taken a lot out of me, physically and mentally.

In April I took a few months off to recover. I needed to spend time catching up with myself and reconnecting with friends and family. Then in June it was back to work modelling and casting for new TV projects ready for 2008. I interviewed for all the top reality shows such as ITV's *Hell's Kitchen* and *I'm A Celebrity... Get Me Out Of Here!* I also continued to work for *Playboy* and all the regular magazines. During the show, I managed to get on the front cover of *OK! Magazine* and that helped my profile considerably.

During this period I also fell deeply in love. A few months into *WAGs Boutique*, I met Lee through a mutual friend and, although I'd been attracted to him, I was still getting over Michael and I couldn't imagine getting involved with someone else at that time. It was March 2007 when things really kicked off between us, but I was incredibly busy with the final few weeks of the programme and had little time for dating as it was. Then Lee invited me out for dinner one night and I realised I actually wanted to spend more time with him.

Lee was special: he wasn't into the celebrity scene – he was much more down to earth, funny, and of course he was, and is, very handsome! We clicked and, without wanting to go into too much detail and jinxing the unique relationship we have together, we became inseparable after our second dinner date.

Unlike all my past boyfriends, I can finally imagine a future with Lee. One thing that makes us gel perfectly is the fact that he and I want the same things from life and from the relationship. We both want to get married and have kids. And we're from the same sort of backgrounds and have grown up without our fathers, so we both understand any insecurities and shortfalls that may stem from that. For example, I constantly need cuddles from Lee, just as I'd had from Papa all those years ago, so he often hugs me for hours. He knows exactly what I need and I love that feeling of warmth and security that I get from those moments with him. Then there's the trust that I've finally learned to feel: for me, this is such a positive element. Lee has shown me a love that is unconditional and pure, and it's that love that allows me to trust him. I have also learned not to cast him in the same mould as my past boyfriends, or even Papa, because Lee isn't them. I've learned it's important not to bring past relationship issues into a new one.

As for Papa, I haven't forgotten what he did, but I have let it go and I want to forget about the past. Although he didn't respond to the letter I wrote to him when I was 18, I think he knew he'd messed up, and so, after five years of silence, he eventually tried to make friends with me again. I'd heard through Ben that Papa wanted to see me so I spent time thinking about it and asked Ben for his number. I remember having to dial it a few times because I was nervous. I'd dial, hang up and then redial. I was so full of trepidation, but Papa obviously saw the number and quickly called me back. As we chatted that day, I swallowed my pride and told Papa that I wanted to see him. I travelled to Spain and we were reunited.

Of course it felt nice when Papa hugged me at the airport and then welcomed me into his home. That day he was remorseful and he said he knew that he hadn't done the best for me, but that he still wanted to be my friend. I felt comforted by that, but, to this day, I still don't know how Papa will fit into my life now because I don't need him any more. I know he's there and that feels good, but I can never forget the past. I'm starting to forgive Papa and I do want to give him a chance at this new friendship we have. Now he rings me up and texts and we are friends, but it will never be like it should have been.

I'm now able to see my stepfather as my real father because I realise that Patrick is the one who has always been there for me. Quite recently, I also realised that it was time to accept that, although Patrick is not my biological father, he *is* my true father. Saying that, at the same time I now feel loved by my family and my new man, too, and for the first time in my life I can actually love myself. I'm thankful for my family and the support they give. I know true friends are very hard to find in this world, but once you find them it's so important not to lose them, but family will always be the most important thing to me. I would die for any one of mine! In fact, I can't wait to start my own family now and, for me, that will be my biggest achievement.

When I think about the bullying I endured, I can now say to other girls who are bullied that there is always a light at the end of the tunnel. It's a phase that many children go through, and, although it doesn't happen to everyone, life is full of those difficult times when you feel vulnerable and lost. The great thing is that these moments always make you stronger. I still experience bullying sometimes, but it's a different type and I know now how to say no. Normally, it rears its ugly head when people try to bully me into doing things with them or for them. I never stood up to the bullies when I was younger, but, if I come across it now, then Lee will always tell me to stand up for myself – and I do. It's only now that I know I have to force myself to be stronger, otherwise I know I will suffer again, like I did all those years ago.

In my early days as a model, I always remember the other models that tried to intimidate me on my first-ever Page 3 at Jeany's studio. But situations like that don't faze me any more. Not only am I resilient to this type of behaviour, but I also don't waste any emotion on it. I don't feel anger or resentment towards girls like them because I know everyone is capable of making mistakes and mistreating other people, and those actions are normally a result of our own insecurities.

When I look back on my experiences in the glamour industry, I wish I'd had more support and guidance from the experts. I also know that, if things had been different with Papa and I hadn't been bullied at school, then perhaps I wouldn't have felt such a pull towards the party world and I might not have had such a desperate need to belong somewhere. I think my journey became more difficult because of my childhood, but it was worsened because I didn't have anyone of any stature in the business to turn to at that time. There are hundreds of compassionate and capable model agents out there, but it's time for them to really take the bull by the horns and start looking after their girls properly! Luckily, I learned from the mistakes I made and in the end I managed to get out of it all. I haven't touched drugs since I was 21 and, although I will always regret taking them, I'm thankful that someone special came along, who showed me how to move on and how to enjoy life in a different way. Now I know there are good people out there and I was so lucky to find one when I needed him.

Writing this book has meant that I can at least try to raise awareness within the glamour industry. There are so many exceptional girls out there who are talented and beautiful, but because they might not have a strong personal support network they will be thrown to the wolves in the same way as I was. If you're young, impressionable and vulnerable, being left to your own devices just doesn't work out there. I think it's time for agents who sign up young models to take more care of them. Many girls ruin their health, their minds and their chances of success mainly through their abuse of drugs, being led astray by the sleazy party scene, falling prey to rogue agents and by opting for soul-destroying jobs like escorting when money becomes tight. On the topic of drugs, I think a girl is either going to try drugs or not, but, if someone could explain the dangers and long-term damage of drug abuse to models out there, this might make them think twice. When you get into drug-taking, it's a slippery slope. You begin to act out of character and it becomes so difficult to recognise yourself and to pull yourself out. Taking drugs is just not worth it.

It's a tough world out there as a glamour girl and the press know and thrive on that. Someone really needs to watch out for the media snakes that are always out there waiting in the shadows to bite. When I read stories about other models and celebrities, I wish people would stop feeding the mouths of these ruthless people. A lot of what they write is rubbish and sometimes I wonder how these people sleep peacefully at night.

As far as I'm concerned, I'm proud of the person I am now. Without having gone through what I did, I wouldn't have become this woman and so I now feel OK about the path I took and the decisions I made along the way. I've had difficult moments and lost my direction, but somehow I have always managed to cope and to get myself back on track. I have a new start now and I'm taking it. Funnily enough, I recently parted company with my manager Chrissie but I picked myself up and moved on! Now, I'm just grateful that I can use my experiences and mishaps to bat these people aside.

Finally Me

When they read my words, other girls may recognise themselves and perhaps they might feel inspired by what I've accomplished. As a starting point, I'll always say that it's important to remain genuine and kind. Coupled with the right support and guidance, a girl can continue to believe in, and follow her precious dreams. Success is possible within this dog-eat-dog industry, and, like the Cameo agent said to me all those years ago, 'Keep your head down and be yourself!'